"Take me to the San"

"The strength of this book is the variety of the authors and their research and close association with the now Sydney Adventist Hospital. The stories may bring laughter, tears, concern and joy or various other emotions—overall, I was inspired."

—Glenn Townend, Chairman, Adventist HealthCare

"The San started as a small cottage hospital but developed into the largest private hospital in New South Wales, providing state-of-the-art services in all aspects of medicine. In my view, the philosophy of a faith-based institution has taken this excellence of care to another dimension as an important component of the healing process."

—Dr Ross Walker, Consultant Cardiologist, author and health media presenter

"Working at the San as a surgeon for 38 years (1964-2001), I came to greatly admire and respect the qualities of the staff, which I regarded as providing an outstanding hospital experience. The empathy and skill of those caring for patients was of the "Nightingale" standard, and the professional respect between nursing and medical staff was unique."

—Mark Killingback, AM, MS (Hon), FACS (Hon), FRACS, FRCS, FRCS (Ed), retired surgeon

"Take me to the San"

STORIES FROM A HOSPITAL WITH A MISSION

Edited by **Branimir Schubert** and **Denise Murray**

SIGNS PUBLISHING
Established 1885

Copyright © 2019 by Adventist HealthCare Ltd.

Copyright of the individual chapters remains with the respective authors. The authors assume full responsibility for the accuracy of all facts and quotations as cited in this book.

Unless otherwise indicated, all Bible quotations are from the Holy Bible, King James Version.

Proudly published and printed in Australia by
Signs Publishing
Warburton, Victoria.

This book was
Edited by Nathan Brown
Proofread by Lindy Schneider and Nathan Brown
Cover design by Shane Winfield
Photographs courtesy of Sydney Adventist Hospital
Typeset in Berkeley Book 11.5/15

ISBN (print edition) 978 1 925044 90 4
ISBN (ebook edition) 978 1 925044 91 1

Contents

Foreword 1
   Dr Branimir Schubert

Preface 3
   Philip D Currie

History: The San and its Mission 7
   Associate Professor Paul Race and Dr Herbert E Clifford
   with Annette Baldwin and Rose-Marie Radley

Does Mission Matter? 22
   Philip D Currie

Medical Influence 37
   Dr Herbert E Clifford and Dr Warren Millist

Nursing Influence 63
   Dr Alex S Currie, Dr Alan Gibbons and Annette Baldwin

San Giving: A Reciprocal Experience 88
   Philip D Currie with Patrina McLean

Chaplaincy and Spiritual Care 97
   Dr Branimir Schubert, Stenoy (Steve) Stephenson
   and Dr Alex S Currie

Mission Shapes our Vision for the Future 120
   Brett Goods

Editorial Team 136
Authors and Contributors 137

Foreword

This book of stories and reflections from "the San"—Sydney Adventist Hospital—reminds me of another book, written by a physician in the first century. His name was Luke and he authored the gospel bearing his name, the longest gospel in the Bible's New Testament.

The uniqueness of Luke's book is that it was written using extensive research: consulting available sources, then compiling them into a re-telling of a story depicting the birth, life, death and resurrection of Jesus Christ. He reliably passed on the Good News story based on his research.

This book is somewhat similar. It is a re-telling of the story of the mission of the Sydney Adventist Hospital—even today still known fondly to many as "the San"—based on the many stories and vignettes shared by people, and about people, who lived the San's mission, contributing to a hospital that has had an impact on many lives. This is not a chronological and systematic historical narrative, but it uses the motivation and inspiration of individuals and events to illustrate how the mission of the hospital has been fulfilled through its healing and restorative ministry since 1903. It also illustrates how mission inspired individuals, decisions, strategies and the pioneering work that remains the hallmark of the San.

When Phil Currie—then Chief Executive Officer of Adventist HealthCare—asked me to engage in this project, I was enormously grateful we had the foundation on which we could start: the oral and written narrative generously provided by Dr Herbert Clifford, himself a past CEO of the San. His experiences, recollections and visionary leadership provided the initial impetus for this book.

Providentially, others came on board with their contributions, each providing their unique insights. We gathered stories from nurses,

"Take Me to the San"

doctors and administrators, and as we wrestled with how to create "one story" from so many sources, mission themes started emerging. Equally providentially, this book was shaped by an expert editorial team. It is truly the result of a creative and generous contribution of the whole team, passionate to preserve and pass on the mission-motivation and the mission-fulfilment of the San.

Much more could be written and should be written; the San's history and present-day stories are worth preserving. But this is the story of the San's mission, leaving room for others to write other books that need to be written, other names to be remembered and other events to be documented.

I hope you will be inspired by the San's mission: "Christianity in Action—Caring for the body, mind and spirit of our patients, colleagues, community and ourselves." Thousands of lives have been impacted by this mission. May yours be one of them.

Dr Branimir Schubert
Director, Mission Integration
Adventist HealthCare

Preface

Philip D Currie

In 2003, I attended the Sydney Adventist Hospital's centenary celebrations, during which several presenters spoke on aspects of the hospital's history. Former San CEO, Dr Herbert Clifford, was one of the speakers, and he shared a number of stories that he later submitted in writing—and these are retained in the Sydney Adventist Hospital library.

In the years since the centenary, there had been thoughts that, at some time, those stories written and developed for the centenary celebration would be published in a book. While I served as CEO of Sydney Adventist Hospital between 2015 and 2017, I had several conversations with Dr Clifford about this possible project.

Stories are an important way of recording history, and a rich history peppered with illustrations provides a positive foundation on which to build the institution's future. In itself, this was fair reason to consider developing a compilation of San stories. But even more compelling was the need to share why the San exists—its mission. The San's mission gives employees a unity of purpose and shapes how staff provide care. Mission also provides the foundation on which managers and administrators build the organisation, and implement strategies and services. Mission impacts how patients, staff and the community experience the San.

Organisational culture is a result of many contributing elements, including mission, vision, values, systems, processes, principles, beliefs, strategy, cultural mix, environmental influences, patterns of behaviour, leadership and management styles, priorities and behaviour. This eclectic mix of elements guides future behaviour and enables the organisation to achieve what it does, commonly referred to as outputs or outcomes.

"Take Me to the San"

Leaders create strategies, strategies are achieved by people, people's thoughts and actions are guided by the culture in which they work, and finally people's actions lead to outcomes.

The San has been highly regarded throughout its history. It is recognised as a leading private hospital in Sydney, and in Australia more broadly. Dedicated, committed and caring staff work with highly-respected doctors to provide exceptional care. In addition, the San is owned and supported by the Seventh-day Adventist Church, whose emphasis on wholistic health has had a significant influence on the hospital's direction, priorities and culture. The San is part of the network of 527 Adventist hospitals, clinics and medical centres worldwide.[1]

The San has grown significantly over the years and now looks after the healthcare needs of more than 186,000 patients per year, including inpatients, day-only patients and outpatients. It also has a stellar reputation within the community and the broader healthcare industry. In this book, it seemed important to explore mission-driven elements that have contributed to the San's culture, with a view to preserving that which has contributed beneficially. In a hospital setting, retaining a positive culture results in better patient clinical outcomes and a healthier community.

Organisations like the San also have a broader responsibility to their communities. The San is foremost a hospital to provide healthcare, but the socio-cultural impact it has on its community is also significant. As the largest employer in the Ku-ring-gai region—in the northern suburbs of Sydney, New South Wales—with more than 2400 employees and 1100 accredited medical practitioners, the financial compensation to employees alone would make a significant economic and social contribution to individuals and their families. Besides the obvious benefits the San provides its community—high-quality healthcare, employment and amenity—I expect the San's mission and culture have a wider reach, influencing the hearts and minds of its people, not only at work but enriching their personal lives and the way they choose to live beyond the San. Such an impact should not go unnoticed. And re-telling some of the San's stories might also influence others to make a broader social contribution, beyond the San, beyond Australia and around the world.

We connect with stories. Stories have the capacity to influence us personally and contribute to our behaviour. Well-told stories have the potential to reveal, highlight and explore cultural artefacts. In these stories, the artefacts are likely to be beliefs, values, attitudes, themes and mission, which contribute to understanding and creating the broad and mature culture of the San.

Once documented in writing, stories are limitless; their value and use cannot be constrained.

They are not limited by time. Stories can be read or told now or in 100 years, with the potential to create an impact today and in the future.

They are not limited to a person. Anyone has access to these stories and they can be inspired, influenced or use them to influence others.

Documented stories are not limited by breadth of impact. They can be read by one person or 100,000 people. The story can be recounted in a small team meeting or in a conference with thousands of people.

A story is not limited to words on a page. Those who read or hear the stories will add interpretive layers that are not drawn out in the story itself.

For these reasons, a story has immeasurable value, with the potential to impact hearts and minds and the culture of an organisation. As such, any book of stories that might influence positively the health outcomes of a large community is a worthwhile project.

This is why a book of "San stories" is important. This book is a tangible way to recognise the San's long and vibrant history, to reflect on how the San's mission has impacted many people in the past and continues to propel and strengthen the organisation into the future. These stories will continue to be used in various ways in the future to inspire San staff, patients and the wider community. The ultimate purpose of the book, like the San itself, is to show how the San's "Christianity in Action" mission strives to reflect

"Take Me to the San"

Christ's wholistic healing ministry: to help bring healing to our patients, colleagues, community and ourselves—in body, mind and spirit.

1. "2018 Annual Statistical Report: 154th Report of the General Conference of Seventh-day Adventists for 2016 and 2017," Office of Archives, Statistics and Research, page 8, <http://documents.adventistarchives.org/Statistics/ASR/ASR2018.pdf>.

History: The San and Its Mission

Associate Professor Paul Race and
Dr Herbert E Clifford with
Annette Baldwin and Rose-Marie Radley

Looking at the Sydney Adventist Hospital today, it is hard to imagine the hospital has been around for almost the duration of the Australian Federation. The land on which the hospital stands was purchased in 1899[1] and the institution officially opened its doors in January, 1903. Between these two dates, Australia formally gained independence from Britain in January, 1901. Reflecting on this long history, including some of the significant incidents and events that might have been forgotten since that time, underscores the hospital's remarkable history, its unique mission and its commitment to excellence in wholistic patient care.

The San was named the Sydney Sanitarium & Hospital[2] for most of the first 70 years of its life. Despite being renamed Sydney Adventist Hospital after a major renovation in 1973, it is still widely known as "the San". Today, the San is part of the Adventist HealthCare group, which includes Sydney Adventist Hospital, San Day Surgery Hornsby, Sydney Adventist Hospital Pharmacy, and San Radiology and Nuclear Medicine.

The San was built because of a belief that ministering to people was both a humanitarian and a spiritual activity. The leaders of the Seventh-day Adventist Church—which still owns the San—saw that to truly reflect the example set by Christ in caring for people, there was a need to address individuals' needs in a wholistic way. In

His interactions with the communities through which He moved, Christ often first ministered to the physical needs of people—especially addressing ill-health and easing suffering—then moved to other needs the individual might reveal. Thus, as the Seventh-day Adventist Church was being established from the mid-1800s, first in America and then in Australia, optimal health was seen to incorporate the physical, mental and spiritual.

The hospital's mission was embedded in its foundations, even if not stated in the exact words we use today. The San's mission describes a disposition and a commitment to meet the needs of others. It is not the work of one individual but a collective effort to work for the benefit of all humanity. To this end, many individuals, families and groups from across the world contributed to the development of the San and helped fulfil its mission.

Set in these founding notions—what the hospital was to be—was a wholistic approach to healthcare with the distinct goal of health improvement. There is clear evidence of the importance of faith, sacrifice and passion among the early founders of the hospital and in those who followed. There is a consistent theme of willing philanthropy, including those who had little and those who had more. There is emphasis on reaching out to support the community locally and internationally. The San connects in many ways with other institutions throughout Sydney, Australia and the South Pacific, as well as through volunteer surgical outreach teams it coordinates each year. These teams have provided free surgery and skills training to 16 countries around the world.[3]

The San strives for excellence and constantly seeks to improve the services offered to both inpatients and outpatients. It values education, and the enhancement of the skills of its staff and doctors as a way to improve the lives of patients and to develop the workforce for the future. Not surprisingly for a Christian institution, the value of chaplaincy, patient advocacy and family support is seen in the spiritual care services offered, family support through Jacaranda Lodge (onsite emergency accommodation) and the services provided by the San's extensive volunteer team.

History: The San and Its Mission

Wholistic focus on health was a key aspect of the early Seventh-day Adventist Church. When services began among Adventist church members in Australia in the late 1800s, care of the sick became a significant part of their work within the community. The initial foray into treatment centres was a small hydrotherapy cottage in inner Sydney devoted to providing treatments to those in need. One vigorous promoter of this approach—Ellen White, an early pioneer of the Adventist church—came from the United States. She determined the role of health institutions to be both preventative and curative in their approach. As demand for healthcare grew, so too did the recognition that facilities and services in the hydrotherapy cottage needed to expand. This culminated in the decision to build the Sydney Sanitarium on the land where Sydney Adventist Hospital is now situated.

From the earliest planning, there was a distinct intention to practise wholism in the care of patients; to ensure the focus was not only on curative medicine, but also on health promotion. In those days, hospitals were usually located in the centre of established population areas, but the San was to be different. Part of the therapy was related to the peaceful, quiet and regenerating environment. Therefore, location—a bushland setting away from the city—was critical. When the location for the new hospital was chosen in 1899, it served that purpose well. Although the San is only 25 kilometres from the centre of Sydney, it was a rural location at that time.

In the following, Dr Herbert Clifford, a former CEO of the San, provides insight into the time and place in which the San was born. The San was indeed "in the bush" when it was first built.

> Within weeks of landing at Sydney Harbour with the First Fleet in 1788, Admiral Arthur Phillip, the first governor of New South Wales, explored an area of Sydney now named the "North Shore". Looking north from what is now the suburb of Gordon—not far from where the San is located—Governor Phillip saw "a land covered with endless wood". A number of reports indicate that by and large the trees were then much bigger. Blackbutts of 9

feet (2.75-metre) diameter were described, with giant eucalypts as well. The heavily forested surroundings of the Lane Cove River were the primary source of timber for the building of early Sydney. Sawpits dotted the landscape, and bullock drays plied tracks to Fiddens Wharf for shipment downriver and across Sydney Harbour. The area was infamous for its lawlessness; fighting among occupiers and against authority was common. From the late 1800s, the timber industry waned, giving way to the "orchardist" period, with oranges, pears, nectarines, peaches and melons the main produce.

It was a 75-acre (approximately 30 hectares) tract of this land in Wahroonga that was seen as ideal by those charged with looking for a suitable site for a new hospital in 1899.

The Adventist church pioneer, Ellen White, was decisive in the founding and development of the San. Looking for funds, she turned to the support of the Wessels family in South Africa. The Wessels family owned a farm on which diamonds were found in the great Kimberley diamond rush of the 1870s; they sold the farm for an immense sum. One of the Wessels family, Pieter, became a church member on meeting an itinerant American Seventh-day Adventist on the South African diamond fields. Pieter's brother, John, and the family followed. They gave much support to building up the Adventist Church in South Africa and other countries around the world, including the United States and Australia.

John Wessels met Ellen White during a visit to America. They became close friends; she regarded John as a son. She asked him to help with the search for a suitable site to build a "Sanitarium" in Sydney; he was central to finding and securing the land on which the San was built. This is clear from Ellen White's own letters: "John Wessels kept searching until he found the place we have bought.

The owner wished to sell out and go to England. In this tract there is seventy-five acres. . . . It has fifteen acres of orchard, bearing abundantly all kinds of fruit, a neat little cottage of four rooms, and woodland. . . . [We] all decided that it would be wise to purchase this place." Further on in the same letter, Ellen White wrote: "Yesterday John wrote us a letter stating that the bargain was closed. We now breathe freely. We feared there might be some impediment [to buying the land], but the business is now settled. We have prayed much over the matter, and we believe that the Lord has directed."[4]

It was on this principal tract of 75 acres that the new Sanitarium hospital was to be built. According to another Ellen White letter, dated November 1, 1899, the price paid was £2200. "Brother Wessels writes that he has taken steps to secure the place. . . . This is the one that will serve our purpose best, and the terms are easy. One hundred pounds is to be paid down, and two hundred, I believe, in three months; the balance in twelve months at five per cent interest."[5] It is thought John Wessels contributed £1000 from his own funds toward the land purchase, although a supporting document has not been located.

The establishment of the San was not without difficulties. Finance was very limited and many decisions were made in faith. Persistence, commitment and passion saw the project move from dream to reality, despite many obstacles. The original hospital building was designed by Dr Merritt Kellogg,[6] a carpenter and physician from the United States, half-brother of Dr John Harvey Kellogg, originator of Kellogg's Corn Flakes. Many who contributed to the building of the San did so from a deep belief in serving their community. Philanthropy came in various forms: contributing from church members' own limited funds, providing volunteer labour, giving produce for fundraising or materials for building work. We see acknowledgment of this generosity across the campus with San structures named for pioneers, visionaries and contributors.

"Take Me to the San"

The building of the hospital progressed slowly, hampered by limited funds. When it was completed, it was three storeys high, 153 feet (47 metres) long by 48 feet (15 metres) wide—excluding verandahs—and built entirely of wood. The building, land and furnishings combined cost $70,000, with $30,000 raised in donations leaving an indebtedness of $40,000.[7]

When the San opened in 1903, it was referred to as the "Home of Health". There was demand for its services even before its doors opened. An extract from the magazine *Australasian Record* in 1955 recounted the story of the San's first admission:

> The first patient was admitted before the San was officially opened, but who was to know that this act of kindness would also be the first occurrence of fulfilling the mission the hospital was set up to achieve. A local Wahroonga shopkeeper had contracted rheumatic fever and, despite many medical consultations, he was advised he had no hope of surviving the illness and would likely pass away within 48 hours. In desperation, the family brought him to the incomplete Sanitarium through what were then bush tracks down Ada Avenue [in the suburb of Wahroonga]. Pleading from the family led to him being admitted, and he surprised even the hospital staff by surviving the illness. . . . Descendants from that family, the Butler family, contributed significantly to the hospital, with one being a key medical consultant at the San for many years.[8]

From these beginnings, the story of the San is one of continuous development and growth. Dr Clifford recalls some of the hospital's significant early milestones:

> When the San opened on January 1, 1903, it had a capacity of 70 beds. A new wing—later to be named for benefactor Shannon—was added to the main building in 1920, enlarging bed capacity to 104. In 1933, a new building including a surgical wing with two surgical wards, two new operating theatres and 14-bed maternity unit was added, to take over the function of the cottage

History: The San and Its Mission

named "Bethel", which had been built in 1915. This cottage still remains onsite as the hospital's Museum.

The next major development at the San was in response to the need to replace the original wooden hospital building—then 70 years old. The reasons for complete replacement of a building of considerable architectural merit have been topics of debate, but there were shared imperatives. Of first importance was the securing of the best patient care into the future. Aesthetically pleasing and admired as it was, the old building could simply no longer support the physical requirements of a contemporary hospital, let alone one destined for leadership in the industry. Inadequacy of the timber framework to carry new diagnostic and therapeutic installations was just one of many deficiencies. The same framework, 70 years old and dry as tinder, was considered by authorities to be Sydney's single major fire hazard. Against a history of several destructions-by-fire of similar buildings, it remains remarkable that this unique structure survived for so long.

The San entered this phase of development in 1968, with completion in 1973. This time it was not thousands of dollars that were required, but millions. This was the development of what is today known as the Clifford Tower, the brick multi-storey building that dominates the view of the hospital from Wahroonga's Fox Valley Road. Dr Clifford recalls some aspects of the transition from the stately old wooden structure to the new hospital:

> Apart from the need to replace the old wooden hospital from a fire-safety perspective, a further imperative of great importance to the San—with its emphasis on quality and personalisation of care—was the need to broaden the clinical base to ensure the hospital could continue to meet the requirements of patient care and nurse education into the future. To that end, when I joined the San administration in 1968, I was advised by the then Chairman of the Board that the San was not expected

to "make money". It was, he counselled, an institution to offer a healing ministry of special quality and to train health professionals.

Inevitably, the building proposal that emerged after two years of planning was a compromise between the ideal and the affordable. When advanced sketches for the main nine-storey building were costed, estimates came in at $9 million, approaching double the budgeted ceiling of $5.5 million for the entire project. As a result, upon review, every choice and option was canvassed. Many proposed refinements were dropped. While these adjustments were regretted at the time, they could also be celebrated among the initiatives that made the new development possible. The priority was that nothing would be permitted to compromise the level of care to be delivered at the bedside.

While the revised plans brought estimates within budget limits, inflationary growth in building costs and later commissioning expenses eventually took the ultimate cost of the project to more than $9 million dollars, the figure once considered impossible. Historically, the San's annual earnings—above expenses—were modest, so the Adventist Church, through its own resources, offerings and contributions from sister organisation the Sanitarium Health Food Company, anticipated carrying the major burden of rebuilding costs. While the hospital administration believed its finance plan to be realistic, it sought provision for a bank loan of $2 million dollars as a contingency measure. Such a loan required security, which the church was not able to provide. The solution was to seek government backing.

At the time, Harry Jago was Minister for Health in the New South Wales state government. A powerful man—in presence, build and manner—he had once been an employee of the nearby Turramurra branch of the Bank of

New South Wales, where the San had done its banking. Harry Jago had also served as Mayor of Ku-ring-gai municipality. As Health Minister, he regularly visited the San, referring to it as "my hospital". It was through Harry that government backing for a rebuilding loan for the major upgrade to the San was secured, unprecedented as it was. However, the projected loan was never drawn; as a not-for-profit institution with new and expanding services, the hospital entered an era of augmented earnings.

With such a long history, the San's growth and development occurred amid the significant expansion of Sydney's suburbs, through various political climates, and spanned momentous world events including the World Wars. These sometimes-distant events impacted even on a hospital in a peripheral suburban area of Sydney. But for a "Christianity in Action" God-ordained cause, seemingly disparate events and activities can come together for good.

These stories reflect the importance of community engagement. The San has a long history of serving the community in numerous ways, of forming long-lasting relationships with local organisations and with key leaders of professional and government bodies. Such relationships can be beneficial, as illustrated in the following example recounted by Dr Clifford:

> The planning and construction process for the new multi-storey hospital took a number of years, from 1968 to 1973. The earliest sketches for the new hospital anticipated a low, spread-out building to accommodate the prevailing convention, meaning no building to rise above the arboreal canopy. But this proposal was rejected by senior architects appointed to the new building project. It was considered that logistical, operating, safety and convenience requirements of a modern hospital called for a vertical rather than horizontal design axis.
>
> However, at a meeting of the local council on April 27, 1970, when approval of this radical redesign of the main San building was sought, Council rejected the application

on account of the planned height of the building, unprecedented in Ku-ring-gai at that time. But San representatives who attended the meeting learned of other objections. A view had been expressed that an enlarged hospital was not really needed and might well become a municipal embarrassment!

At a time of high inflation, estimates of the cost of the hospital building project were escalating by thousands of dollars a day. This concern was confronting enough, aside from the prospect of reassembling planning teams to work through months of revision and redrafting.

One morning, a call from the Ku-ring-gai mayor indicated that plans for the hospital had ongoing resistance and would likely not be approved. Lobbying, he suggested, was the only option. A date for a site inspection was nominated by Council. San representatives met delegates on the front lawn of the grounds.

One Councillor most vocally opposed to the new project did not attend this group inspection. He became the focus of our next endeavour, accepting an invitation to a "private" visit of the site. During that meeting, both the Councillor and a hospital representative noticed ex-service badges on each other's lapels. As old soldiers do, they began to reminisce, finding points of shared experience. The Councillor reflected on his time in a Japanese prisoner-of-war camp. He recounted how he had lived for months on token rice rations. With deep feeling, he described his growing weakness, shortness of breath, swelling of legs and body, and how his vision began to fade and he felt life ebbing away. These were symptoms of advanced beri-beri—thiamine (vitamin B1) deficiency—caused by his limited diet.

At the time, the Red Cross in Australia was active in sending food and comfort packages to prisoners in these camps. One item included in parcels to selected camps was Marmite, a savoury paste similar to Vegemite, for spreading on bread or toast. The clever rationale behind the Red Cross' choice to include Marmite in parcels was that, as an acquired taste, it was unlikely to be attractive to captors; at the same time, it was a nutritious source of thiamine, the anti-beri-beri vitamin. Australian prisoner-leaders in the camp carefully doled out the precious "medicine": two teaspoons of Marmite per day to the worst afflicted. Fast forward to the meeting at the San that day, the Councillor described how that during weeks of "Marmite therapy" his swelling subsided, his strength returned and his vision brightened.

After he shared this story with us, there was a pause. Then I ventured, "Councillor, do you know who makes Marmite?"

"No," he said, "I just knew it was sent to the prisoner-of-war camps by the Red Cross."

"Well," I said, "we do—Sanitarium; Sanitarium makes Marmite, it's our sister company!"

There was a profound pause. The Councillor's face first blanched, then flushed. "You make Marmite?" As we assured him it was true, his eyes glistened and tears began to trickle down his cheeks.

Then abruptly he said, "Gentlemen, I must go." Despite not yet having discussed the proposed hospital plans, he left. Hospital representatives did not know what to think of this hasty departure. Here was an influential and opposed representative of Council, who had twice avoided or missed an opportunity to review the plans for the new hospital building, or even engage in constructive dialogue on the proposals. Was he disinterested, was his mind set in opposition? How could he be reached now?

"Take Me to the San"

The next meeting of Council again found San representatives in the Council chamber's public gallery, anxious and not knowing what to expect. There had been no feedback from our lobbying endeavours, and no opportunity to present the hospital's case to the central figure in opposition to the San project. The Councillor concerned spoke early in the meeting. Addressing the mayor and fellow councillors, he stated that he had reviewed the development proposal and considered that the plans responded to the need for a new facility in the best and only possible way. "Change of their plans is unnecessary, and any further delay unwarranted. The project," he asserted, "should be approved at this meeting." It was an extraordinary turnaround from one who had previously been the most vocal opponent of the San's redevelopment.

With council approval finally granted, construction on the new hospital building commenced. Replacement of the historic but aged, creaking and fire-prone San building with a nine-storey structure with twice the capacity was a salutary development. The new building stood immediately in front of the old. With preparations completed, transfer of patients was undertaken in one day and demolition of the old building soon followed. Dr Clifford reflects on this new era for the San:

The new hospital was a singular innovation in the New South Wales private health industry and indeed in Australia. Completed in 1973, the rebuilding project opened the way for the San—already a cherished community healthcare institution—to transition from a Sanitarium model into that of the comprehensive modern hospital. Interested in inspecting its features, health operatives in all disciplines visited in a steady stream over the following months.

Impressive as the new facilities were, the physical changes and innovations were simply the ground on which a new expanse of general and speciality services were to grow. Up to that time, private hospital services were limited largely to the realm of the regular and the routine. In the decade following rebuilding, the San was transformed into a modern healthcare institution with a comprehensive range of medical, surgical and supporting services, and wide outreach into the community and beyond.

In the 21st century, private hospitals have further enlarged their services, approaching in some instances those of the "Teaching Hospital"—a status traditionally held by public hospitals. Indeed, in the past decade, the San has undergone further major developments and has a clinical school of Sydney University Faculty of Medicine with in-hospital clinical placements for doctors, physiotherapists and allied health. This is in addition to the long-standing nurse education program offered in conjunction with Avondale College of Higher Education, a sister organisation to the San. The San has played an innovative and leading role in this national development in healthcare, and is upholding its mission to continually find ways to advance its health and healing services.

Nostalgia for the past and unease with change are inevitable. Departure from "the blueprint" is a phrase sometimes expressed, reflecting deep attachment to historical roots. But the steadfast reality is that Christian ministry and outreach are above method and modality; they have to do with ideals and values. These ideals and values can operate in any generation, and in models of institution and organisation most fitting to the time.

One example illustrates this point: in the 1960s—before the San's rebuilding—the average length of patient stay at the San exceeded 10 days. For many patients, it was two or three weeks; and for some patients, months. That latitude in today's economy would not be permitted by government, not supported by private health funds, nor could the required premiums be afforded. Many surgical operations—for which hospital stay was once several days—are now undertaken on an outpatient or day-patient basis. There is added advantage: early return home is shown to carry less risk, enhance recovery and save costs. That is surely a winning strategy for patients.

While technical innovation and advances in clinical areas have strong appeal, arguably the more significant developments of the time were those in organisation, both in hospital administration and medical staffing. In the organisational sphere, emphasis was placed on participation, delegation, consultation, policy elaboration and structured review. In the staffing realm, key features included formal accreditation procedures, the granting of doctors' visiting privileges, consultative mechanisms, and collective activity through quality management and the rostering of services where appropriate. At the San, such developments—novel to private hospitals of the time and introduced despite considerable opposition—provided a foundation for exercise of the clinical disciplines in a productive and secure environment and with the most favourable outcomes.

From its commencement, the San has striven to fulfil its mission to offer the best care for its time, through services underpinned by a commitment to excellence, integrity, dignity and compassion. With more effective medicines, refined anaesthesia, minimal-trauma surgery and early return to activity, contemporary healthcare practice has changed significantly from the "R&R" approach of the early 1900s, when patients came to the San for extended periods of rest, relaxation, massage, hydrotherapy, diet and exercise. Yet the San continues to offer high-quality, evidence-based healthcare, including a focus on health promotion, enhancement of lifestyle through education, and recovery through rehabilitation.

1. Ellen White, Letter 171, 1899.
2. Originally built as the "Sydney Sanitarium", the hospital was renamed "Sydney Sanitarium and Hospital" in 1910 when registered under the Private Hospitals Act. "Sanitarium" is an American term applied in the mid-19th century to health-recovery institutions and resorts. Natural forms of therapy were most favoured.
3. Open Heart International: <https://ohi.org.au/our-impact/>.
4. Ellen White, Letter 171, 1899.
5. Ellen White, Letter 190, 1899.
6. <https://www.sah.org.au/our-history>.
7. General Conference Bulletin, April 12, 1903, page 175.
8. "The Sydney Sanitarium's First Patient," *Australasian Record*, July 4, 1955.

Does Mission Matter?

Philip D Currie

In an environment where we seem to have a preoccupation with branding buzzwords and marketing jargon, hundreds of millions of dollars are sometimes spent on building an "identity" for a company or organisation.[1] So it's easy to become cynical or, at least, blasé about what an organisation claims to stand for.

But the ability to articulate why an organisation exists—what its fundamental purpose is—is important. An organisation's "mission" endeavours to do that.

Mission gives employees unity of purpose, working together for the common goal and a common good. Mission provides the framework from which leaders and managers build the organisation, innovate and grow into the future. Mission also communicates, to those in the broader community who interact with it, what the organisation stands for. Mission helps shape the attitudes and behaviours of individuals and the organisation's culture as a whole, which directly impacts outcomes.

In 2002, the leadership team at the San set about to more clearly define and articulate the San's mission. At that time, the hospital had a mission statement that stretched to a number of pages. Then-CEO of the San, Dr Leon Clark wanted to condense it into a short phrase that all staff could relate to and remember. Senior hospital leadership met for a weekend of workshopping, presentations, discussions and prayer. During that weekend, there were many ideas but none seemed inspired nor seemed to resonate with the whole team.

Does Mission Matter?

Late on the final day, Dr Clark suggested the words "Christianity in Action". It was like the team had an epiphany. Everyone agreed they were the words that best reflected the San's values, its reason for existence and ongoing purpose. The team challenged these three words from various perspectives, giving rigor to our debate. By the close of the session, the team unanimously supported updating the San's mission statement to "Christianity in Action".

This phrase had been used around the hospital for some time. The previous San CEO, Mr Ian Grice, supported by Mrs Pam Ludowici—Chaplain and Manager of the Help Team Volunteers—had revitalised the San's team of volunteers. These volunteers were given lanyards to secure name tags, and printed on the lanyard was the phrase "Christianity in Action".

So these words had gained some traction, but it was only near the conclusion of Dr Clark's workshopping weekend that these words came to him as a potential new mission statement for the San. These words represented the essence of the San and its mission. During Jesus' ministry on earth, He related to people through healing and teaching. The San's leadership felt the hospital's role had always been—and would continue to be—that of extending the healing ministry of Jesus to others. By helping people heal, we follow His example and demonstrate "Christianity in Action".

Following the workshopping weekend, an extensive communications campaign commenced to promote the new mission statement. The objective was for all staff to not only remember but to reflect the San's mission in their day-to-day care.

Staff surveys showed that the new mission statement was well received, with 80 per cent of staff indicating they supported the statement. Although this response was good, we wanted greater buy-in. The same survey revealed 20 per cent of staff did not easily identify with the mission statement on the basis they didn't have a Christian background. So further thought was given to the mission statement. "Christianity in Action" was expanded to include the phrase "Caring for the body, mind and spirit of our patients, colleagues, community and ourselves." When this was released, staff survey results showed 96 per cent of staff supported it. The mission statement had incredible traction.

At the most basic level, a hospital's overt focus is to heal the body. But more than that, the San's mission reflects the Seventh-day Adventist philosophy of wholism, recognising that humans are complex, integrated beings comprised of body, mind and spirit, with each one of these elements influencing the others. From the beginning of Adventist forays into healthcare, its hospitals around the world integrated into their philosophy the need to care for patients' physical, mental and spiritual needs. The San has been doing this since 1903. The new mission statement more clearly articulates wholism and the commitment with which it is delivered.

Mission matters because mission influences the culture of an organisation, and culture influences patient outcomes. By sharing personal stories and some experiences patients have recounted over the years, we can see how the San's mission is more than mere words on paper, it is being lived out each day. The San is a place where people can experience Christianity in Action, where patients, colleagues, community and ourselves are cared for physically, mentally and spiritually.

Mission influences culture

When inducting new staff to the San and talking with the hospital leadership team about the San's mission, I would often say, "Christianity in Action is 'Christ in Action'. If you want to understand 'Christ in Action', observe what Jesus did, what motivated His actions and how He behaved. That is Christianity in Action."

Records suggest that Jesus spent much of His time healing people physically. But His ministry also incorporated healing people mentally and spiritually. Teaching was also part of His ministry; He taught whenever the opportunity presented itself, whether to masses of people at once or on an individual basis.

The San incorporates Jesus' approach of healing and teaching in its mission. This includes caring for physical needs and helping the

Does Mission Matter?

body to heal; providing psychological support; improving the mind, knowledge and skills through teaching and education; and providing the opportunity for people to connect with what brings meaning and purpose to them personally—caring for their spiritual needs.

For each person working at the San, our commitment to mission has the capacity to impact us personally and influences our behaviour. If we do this, the care we give will be exemplary; we will endeavour to be a responsible and consultative employer; the services we provide will meet the needs of our community; our interactions with contractors and suppliers will be ethical; and we will strive to keep ourselves healthy. In this way, living our mission, as individuals, contributes to the collective organisational behaviour.

A patient's hospital experience is not only about the facilities or the technology, tests and procedures. A patient's experience is inextricably linked to the actions of those who care for them. The San's mission encourages a culture of caring more, meaning we strive to connect authentically with others and seek to meet their needs. It means each of us holds ourselves accountable for our actions. It means we respect and empower our patients and colleagues, and we work hard to serve the needs of our community.

A culture of caring makes a difference not only to a patient's experience and their recovery, but also whether they choose to come to the San:

> In 2017, I visited a patient who had been in our intensive care unit for quite some time and was recovering on the wards. As we chatted, Paul[2] shared with me some of what he'd been through.
>
> "I had been feeling unwell at home, but I wasn't sure what the problem was. I got to a point where I felt seriously unwell. Even though I live one-and-a-half hours from the San, I said to my wife, 'Just take me to the San.' We got in the car and came here. I had this feeling that if I didn't get to the San, there was a high possibility that I might die."
>
> After Paul shared with me the cause of his illness, the many

weeks in intensive care and his long road to recovery, he said, "I think I was right; without the San's care, I probably wouldn't be here."

Paul had suffered from septic shock, an infection that causes serious illness and has the potential to have a deadly outcome. But what makes this story even more powerful is that Paul is a medical specialist who had previous interactions with the San. He lives close to a major teaching public hospital. He could have elected to go there or to any of at least 15 other public or private hospitals that were closer to him than the San. Just visualise Paul, incredibly sick, just wanting to get to hospital to get treatment, yet he chose to travel past other hospitals to go to the San. His intimate knowledge of medicine and the San meant that he chose to put his life in the hands of the San in his time of health crisis.

Paul's story is a powerful illustration of the impact an organisation's mission can have on its culture. The mission is nurtured and promoted through staff, management and leadership, and is constantly reinforced. The following examples are like many patient stories I've been privileged to hear over the years:

> During my time as a hospital leader at the San, I met with many people in various settings who mentioned they or a family member had been a patient at the San. At one function in Sydney, I sat next to a gentleman I'd not previously met. As we introduced ourselves, I discovered he had a legal background and operated a company providing services throughout Australia. Although his family was based in Sydney, they spent weekends and holidays in places such as Orange and the Hunter Valley. This gentleman told me his sons loved to ride motorbikes. He said that on a number of occasions after his sons had motorbike accidents, he had bundled them into the car, driving two or three hours to the San to get the healthcare they valued and trusted.

On another occasion, I met an older gentleman who, after finding out I worked at the San, declared it was the only hospital he would go to. He lived in Sydney but loved to holiday on the coast, a few hours north of Sydney. "Recently while holidaying on the coast, I experienced chest pain," he told me. "I got in the car and told my wife to drive me to the San."

After asking him how that experience had worked out for him, I suggested to him that chest pain was potentially serious and that the best course of action would be to call an ambulance and seek treatment at the closest hospital! Nevertheless, this story and many like it demonstrate people's sentiment toward the San—it's worth the trip.

People don't choose to keep coming back to an organisation unless their experience is positive. I believe the San's mission has a palpable impact on its culture and the way people are cared for. Mission becomes a mirror that is held up to assess the organisation and how it is performing. Is the espoused mission reflected in employees' behaviours, and organisational culture? Is there an alignment between the mission promise and experience?

The San's mission and the organisational culture also helps recruit people who are aligned with its ethos. I've talked with many of our staff and doctors who heard of the San's Christian heritage, its mission and culture, and made a considered choice to work at the San because it is a hospital aligned with their beliefs, values and attitudes. In this way, the San's culture is further strengthened by people already personally aligned to mission.

For more than a century, the San has developed and nurtured a reputation for being a hospital that not only helps with routine health matters but also the community trusts with their lives. This is a special hospital. The San's exceptional clinicians, nurses and support staff work collaboratively to provide clinical excellence. This is coupled with the attitude to do whatever it takes to give every patient every chance to have the best recovery. Striving for excellence and keeping focused on mission has reinforced a great culture, informed by and emulating "Christianity in Action", and this is what makes people choose the San.

Culture influences patient outcomes

The San has grown significantly over the years and is now responsible for contributing to the healthcare needs of more than 186,000 patients each year. The hospital has a stellar reputation in the community and within the broader healthcare industry. None of this happens by accident.

In 1986, during my second year as a student nurse at the San, I worked on report roster. This meant I didn't have a designated ward but, at the start of my shift, I had to report to the duty manager in the roster office to be sent to any area of the hospital where they needed help. On this particular night-duty shift, I was sent to the intensive care unit (ICU) as they were having a really busy night. I will never forget that shift. While I probably couldn't articulate it as clearly at the time, I learnt one of the most valuable lessons of my career: an organisation's culture really does influence patient outcomes.

> When the duty manager told me I'd be working in ICU, my mind began to race: *I'm only a second-year trainee, I haven't even completed the critical-care component of the nursing course, how can I be any help in ICU?* I expressed these thoughts to the duty manager and he responded, "Yes I know, but they will look after you and they won't ask you to do anything for which you're not trained. You will still be a big help to them." With these reassuring words, I walked nervously to the intensive care unit.
>
> At that time, ICU had 11 beds—seven acute-care beds and four lower-acuity bays. When I arrived, it was change of shift. Nurses for the new shift gathered in the staff station to hear a detailed report on all 11 patients from the outgoing team leader. The ICU was full and, despite my inexperience, it was clear to me that some of the patients

were extremely ill. Gary, the team leader for ICU that night, was looking after one of the sickest patients, Mr Jones. Gary asked me to work alongside him for the shift.

Having received a general handover, staff moved to stations just outside each patient's room and received a more detailed handover. Gary talked me through his routine. First, he read through the patient's chart, and checked the doctors' orders and nurses' entries, all the medication charts and flow charts. This was followed by a thorough clinical assessment of the patient, which included checking all the equipment attached to him. There was a ventilator machine to help the patient breathe, and a number of infusion pumps to deliver fluids and drugs to help the heart pump more effectively and to keep blood pressure within normal parameters.

An intra-aortic balloon pump was in place. This machine was used for patients who were in significant heart failure to give their heart an opportunity to recover from transient failure. Monitors measured a range of signals such as heart rhythms, continuous blood pressure monitoring and central venous pressure lines. Gary checked postoperative X-ray reports to see that the various tubes were in the correct places and checked for fluid on the lungs or air pockets between the lung and chest wall. He reviewed the latest pathology test results and finalised his comprehensive baseline clinical assessment of his patient. After that was completed, we began to settle in to a busy night in ICU.

Sometime later, however, Gary noticed a sudden change in the patient's condition and hit the cardiac arrest alarm. A piercing sound rang out, and staff and doctors from across the ICU descended on Mr Jones' room. As a student nurse, I felt helpless and stood back, observing clinical experts in action as they worked together to try to stabilise the patient. Mr Jones was administered anti-arrhythmic drugs and multiple cardioversions to try to revert his heart back into a life-sustaining rhythm. Nothing seemed to be working and a tense 15 minutes followed. Then the doctor issued an order for a particular drug. One of the registered nurses dashed to the drug cupboard to get it. I asked someone next to me what was happening.

"The doctor has ordered Bretylium to be given," she explained. "It's an anti-arrhythmic agent designed to suppress abnormal rhythms of the heart. Once they give this drug, it will take 15 to 20 minutes to take effect. It's the last-line arrhythmic agent that can be used. If it doesn't work, it's not looking good for this patient."

The intensity of this cardiac arrest was palpable. This life-threatening clinical situation required the care of at least half a dozen staff working with focused attention to do their best for Mr Jones in difficult and deteriorating circumstances. But this was not only a clinical situation. On the bed lay a father, a grandfather, a husband, a brother, a cousin, a friend, a neighbour. This reality grew on me. This was my first cardiac arrest, a clinical event, yet emerging in my mind were the social implications and the effect that a poor outcome would have on his family, friends and loved ones.

Mr Jones continued to deteriorate. But about 20 minutes after the Bretylium was administered, his cardiac rhythm improved and, with one final electrical defibrillation, his heart returned to a life-sustaining rhythm. The immediate crisis was over.

This was the beginning of a long and challenging night. Mr Jones' life hung in the balance. Throughout the night, he continued to go into cardiac arrest. Sometimes the arrest lasted two, five, 10 or 15 minutes and each time the team worked feverishly to bring him back from the brink.

Does Mission Matter?

I lost count of the number of times he arrested—perhaps more than a dozen times. Each time he arrested, the same drill occurred, with a disciplined team coming together with one objective: to give Mr Jones the best chance of survival.

There was no time to feel tired on this night shift. Mr Jones' condition was too critical, needing constant focused attention. At about 5.30 am, in a rare quieter moment and with the patient stable, Gary and I sat for a few minutes while he wrote notes in the patient's chart. I contemplated the night's events.

There was a question in my mind, which I asked Gary: "It seems obvious Mr Jones is really sick and no resource has been spared in treating him in an effort to save his life. But I wonder what chance he really has? Do you think its 50-50 or is it closer to 10-90? What do you think?"

Still in my training, my first shift in ICU and my first observation of a cardiac arrest, it seemed a legitimate question to ask. But Gary took no time to contemplate a response. It was immediate, it was reflex, and it reflected his character and the San's culture. Turning from his paperwork, he looked me straight in the eyes, ensuring I received the full impact of the importance of his response: "My job is not to wonder what chance he's got, but to give him every chance he's got."

It was an epiphany for me. The significance of what Gary said dawned on me. I felt somewhat small for having asked the question, but grateful I had the benefit of such wisdom so early on in my nursing career.

Over the years, I have reflected on that night caring for Mr Jones in ICU and Gary's response. I interpret it on two levels. First, a clinician who contemplates the probability of a patient's recovery needs to ensure this doesn't unduly influence their behaviour toward, or treatment of, that patient. Second, this experience took place in a hospital with a strong Christian foundation. The San's culture is heavily influenced by its "Christianity in Action" mission. The culture is shaped by Christian practices based on biblical principles and prayer. The CEO, senior leaders, managers, doctors, staff, chaplains and volunteers promote a Christian ethos. The values of dignity, integrity and clinical excellence are promoted extensively across the organisation.

The public choose the hospital because it is well known for these values. The San culture is informed—in the context of the Christian story—by a God who gave His best, His only Son, doing whatever it took to save humanity. This guides us to do our best for others. From that memorable night in ICU, I no longer entertained thoughts of the "probability" of a patient's recovery. My patient care was guided by an unwavering commitment to give them every chance.

Throughout the 33 years I worked at the San, I undertook a number of different roles including patient care, education, business development, General Manager and CEO. Frequently, I would meet people or receive letters from patients and family members who were grateful for the care received at the San. A few years ago, I had the privilege of sharing a long conversation with a patient that reaffirmed my belief that the San's mission and culture really do influence patient outcomes.

> I arrived at my office one morning to find a letter that had been slipped under my door. I picked it up, noting my name was handwritten on the envelope. I placed it to one side while I checked emails, but the letter begged to be opened. While I read the letter, I wondered if the patient was still in hospital. Sure enough, he was, so I went to visit him. I always enjoyed the chance to interact with patients and this presented another opportunity. I knocked on his door and introduced myself to Mr Smith.
>
> "It's so good you have come," he said. "I want to tell you what's happened to me." And he launched into explaining what brought him into hospital. "You might be able to tell from my accent that I'm not from Australia. I recently

retired and decided to come to visit my daughter in Australia. Our plan was to come for a little while, enjoy some travelling and catch up with family. On Easter Friday, I went into the bathroom where I slumped on the floor and was quite confused. I wasn't sure what was going on. The ambulance was called and they brought me to your hospital. Arriving in your Emergency Care Unit, the doctors quickly assessed me. I had blood tests and a CT scan and was soon diagnosed with a stroke. Medications were started. When I arrived in hospital, I couldn't move one side of my body at all. This arm and leg wouldn't move and I could barely talk. The emergency team looked after me well and then transferred me to the intensive care unit.

"I remained in ICU for several days," he continued. "I still couldn't use my arm or leg and found it difficult to communicate." Pointing to the side of his mouth, he said, "This side of my mouth wasn't working and I just garbled my words. After several days in intensive care, I had stabilised enough to leave ICU and was transferred to this ward. It is now seven days since I collapsed in my daughter's bathroom. You can see that I'm now moving my leg and arm. I am beginning to walk again and I'm speaking pretty well. There is a little residual weakness on one side, but it's improving all the time."

As he spoke, Mr Smith's passion seemed to increase. "You know, everywhere I have been in this hospital, the staff have cared for me well. The doctors in emergency care quickly diagnosed my stroke and started treatment, and the nurses attended to my needs and encouraged me. The intensive care staff and doctors all cared for me well. And now on the ward, the neurologist, nursing staff, physiotherapists and hospitality staff have all provided great care. They are all attentive and make me feel good." At this point, he looked directly at me and said, "You

"Take Me to the San"

know, I think I'm a pretty good judge of staff within a hospital setting. In my homeland, I have just retired as a dental surgeon after working in hospitals for more than 40 years. I know hospitals well. I know hospital staff—and your team is exceptional."

I felt a sense of pride for the San as Mr Smith spoke about his experience. I know things don't always go well for all patients all the time and we can always improve, but it is a privilege to hear patients speaking positively of their time at the San.

Mr Smith continued, "This experience I've had in your hospital has occurred over Easter. I know you know what Easter represents, but I want you to hear my version. I was raised a Christian but, over the past 45 years, I have not practised Christianity. But I have some background and understanding of it. God sent His Son, Jesus, to this earth to give people a chance at eternal life. Jesus died for us— He was crucified on a cross on Friday. When he died, they took His body down off the cross and placed it in a tomb. A large stone was placed across the entrance of the tomb and guards positioned in front of the tomb to prevent people from stealing His body. Early on Sunday morning, His disciples went to the tomb and found the stone rolled aside and nobody in sight. On making her way out of the tomb, Mary saw someone she thought was a gardener. In her emotional distress, with tears in her eyes, she approached the gardener to ask if he had seen what had happened, and where Jesus' body had been taken."

Mr Smith paused in his recounting of the Easter story, but then he appeared to gain some inner strength and recommenced his version. "It says in the Bible that as Mary looked into the gardener's eyes, she saw Christ."

Drawing another breath, Mr Smith said, "As I have experienced your staff here, I have seen Christ. Whether it was in emergency care, intensive care or on the ward, whether it was doctors, nurses, physiotherapists, hospitality staff, wardsmen or cleaners—I have seen Christ."

I was in some shock. It's hard to describe the thoughts and emotion I felt while I sat there listening to Mr Smith recount the Easter story and share his experience as a patient at the San.

"Easter is a time Christians recognise as symbolic of Jesus' death and resurrection," Mr Smith continued. "I can't help but reflect on the symbolism of my hospital experience over this Easter weekend. Physically, I stroked out; spiritually, I had left Christianity long ago. My hospital experience over Easter has not only healed my body, but my mind and spirit. The symbolism of my healing at the San, and Jesus' healing and resurrection that Easter weekend more than 2000 years ago, has affected me deeply. This experience and your staff's care has given me a refreshed insight into Christianity."

I was very moved, listening to Mr Smith. Never before had I heard a patient recount their experience so eloquently. Mr Smith's story epitomised the San's mission. He had been admitted for a physical ailment—a stroke—and he was leaving hospital healing in body, mind and spirit. I stood there in front of Mr Smith hoping he did not detect the mist forming in my eyes.

Patients experience our mission delivered through our staff in the way we care. For Mr Smith, "Christianity in Action" was experienced in a profound way. The full meaning of our mission and its expression through a caring culture meant he not only had a great outcome physically and mentally, but he was comforted and encouraged spiritually.

Jesus' example of caring for others—"Christ in Action"—is what influences the San at its core. The San's mission conveys what the organisation stands for and why it exists. Mission informs and guides the behaviour of those who work at the San, thus shaping the organisation's culture. A culture of clinical excellence and more care indelibly influences outcomes for our patients, with a flow-on effect on their families, our staff and our community. In this chapter and through patients' experiences like those recounted above, we can see that yes, mission does matter.

1. "Making a statement; a brand's cost versus worth," *Think Marketing*, October 27, 2015, <thinkmarketingmagazine.com/7-most-expensive-logos-world/>.

2. All patient names have been changed and some personal details omitted to maintain privacy.

Medical Influence

Dr Herbert E Clifford and Dr Warren Millist

For more than a century, the San's reputation has been built on the provision of outstanding medical services. This has required vision and innovation; quality and governance; ethics and excellence. This is illustrated in the following stories taken from the experiences of doctors and administrators involved in establishing new services at the San, particularly in the past 50 years. Limited space in this volume restricts the ability to include all the initiatives from all those involved in establishing medical and surgical services at the San since 1903. But we hope these stories will encourage others to share their experience, to demonstrate the enormous effort, dedication, faith and courage of the thousands of skilled people who have helped make the San the centre of excellence it is today—a flagship hospital, living out its mission to serve the community.

Vision and innovation

Perhaps one of the best illustrations of vision and innovation in medical practice at the San was the commencement of cardiac services at the San—a private hospital—at a time when cardiac surgery was the acknowledged and exclusive province of the public hospital sector.

Looking at the range and quality of cardiac services operating at the San today, it is hard to imagine a time when they did not exist.

"Take Me to the San"

The following includes some stories about the less-remembered history of heart surgery at the San: how it went from nothing to being the first private hospital in Australia to offer a comprehensive cardiac program that included diagnostic, medical, surgical and rehabilitation services.

In the following, Dr Herbert Clifford—CEO of the San at the time cardiac services were established—recalls how these services progressed from idea to reality:

> The notion of introducing heart surgery at the San arose out of an exchange, in the mid-1970s, between surgeon colleague Dr Don Wilson and myself. Dr Wilson, an Australian-American, was a San-employed consultant in general surgery. He was also a qualified cardiothoracic surgeon, trained at Loma Linda University Hospital in California. Having performed heart surgery in the private sector in the United States, he saw the potential for its introduction at the San. It was a vision he cherished and shared.
>
> In Australia at the time, with a number of other speciality fields, heart surgery was the exclusive domain of the public hospital system. Consequently, when the San Board was presented with the proposal to introduce cardiac surgery at the San, it adopted a cautious, risk-averse view toward the initiative. Against this backdrop, it took someone of Dr Wilson's experience and personal testimony to strengthen the Board's courage and resolve to proceed with the venture. Dr Wilson's contribution was thus crucial to establishing cardiac services at the San.
>
> A number of factors further motivated the San's entry into this important field. The demand for intervention had outstripped the capacity of the existing cardiac surgery programs in public hospitals. This left a growing number of patients in New South Wales "in suspension" for

lengthy periods. Long waiting lists placed people at risk of further heart attacks or even death.

Again, a cardiac surgery program at the San would afford the opportunity for a wholistic approach to cardiac health: diagnostic, early intervention, surgery if necessary, rehabilitation, and patient education for both inpatients and outpatients. These health-promoting tenets were long-time special interests of the San aligned with its mission.

From the outset, opposition to a San-conducted heart surgery program was broad-based and formidable, both from within and outside the organisation.

Internally, it was felt by some surgeons that the demands of heart surgery—for beds, funds, theatre time and personnel—could compromise activities in their own established fields. It was true that the San's facilities, particularly operating theatres, were already well utilised.

Members of the San Board were concerned about risks, resources and even the place of a heart surgery program in the hospital's mission. Dr Wilson's testimony was salutary in this regard; he pointed out that surgery in this field, rehabilitation and patient education would become significant extensions of the hospital's outreach, mission and influence. In retrospect, we can observe that realisation of those assurances has well exceeded expectations.

At one meeting of the San Board during this time, I was asked whether there were "any risks involved" with a program of this nature. I wished I could have said "no", but of course, there were—and I had to say "yes". The reality is that risk and reward are fellows, and that without venture a cause is doomed to stagnation. Redeeming virtues are always a little courage and a little faith!

"Take Me to the San"

And much hard work! Some of that hard work had started a few years prior with upgrades to infrastructure, equipment and staff training at the San. In the following account, Dr Warren Millist, anaesthetist at the San for 30 years (1964–1994), recalls some of the initiatives at the hospital in the mid-1960s to mid-1970s, many of which laid the foundations for innovations such as the cardiac service.

I arrived at the San in December, 1964, from the Alfred Hospital in Melbourne to work as an anaesthetist. It was standard practice after surgery for patients to remain on trolleys—in the care of a nurse—in the corridor just outside the operating room. The only equipment was an oxygen cylinder and face mask, and the lighting was poor.

As anaesthetists frequently used ether, many of the patients were slow to recover and not fully conscious even when they returned to the ward. On the ward, a nurse was then required to sit with them until they had fully regained consciousness.

It was proposed that a recovery ward should be established in the two-bed room immediately outside the operating theatre, and that this be converted into a properly equipped and staffed recovery ward. Piped oxygen and suction was installed by hospital engineer John Maxwell, and a large Watson Victor monitor and defibrillator was installed. This ward was staffed by registered nurses and was a great improvement in patient safety. As a result of this initiative, the San was the first private hospital in Sydney with a properly equipped and staffed recovery ward.

At the time, every anaesthetist had to bring all their own anaesthetic equipment, including anaesthetic machine, syringes, needles and anaesthetic agents, including cylinders of nitrous oxide. This was a huge burden for the anaesthetist to carry around, let alone ensure that the

Medical Influence

equipment was properly maintained and safe to use. No anaesthetic could commence until all the anaesthetist's equipment had been sterilised by boiling!

The hospital purchased two anaesthetic machines so there would be a standard machine in each of the operating theatres. These machines were serviced by CIG-trained technicians and certified as safe. Oxygen and nitrous oxide were supplied by the hospital. Sterile packs of syringes and needles were prepared, ensuring that the equipment provided was already sterilised, which was better for patient safety and avoided the delay of sterilising the anaesthetist's own syringes. This was another step forward in comparison to other Sydney private hospitals at the time.

About 1966, the hospital also purchased an electrocardiogram (ECG) monitor and two ventilators for visiting anaesthetists to use. This was a substantial cost but another significant advance in patient care.

Around the mid-1960s, each ward had a small steam autoclave, in which syringes, needles, and all other reusable devices were autoclaved and reused. Different wards had different types of syringes and needles that were not necessarily interchangeable. This was confusing for nurses and doctors. I approached administration and suggested that a central sterilising department be set up. This was established and Marjorie Batchelor was the first registered nurse in charge of central sterilising at the hospital. This arrangement ensured that each ward was supplied with sterile and standardised equipment.

There was no hospital-wide protocol or equipment for managing cardiac arrests or similar emergencies on the wards at this time. Defibrillation required that the massive Watson Victor defibrillator had to be brought from the recovery ward to wherever the patient was, which was a difficult and time-consuming task. A new system was implemented whereby small suitcases containing ventilating equipment, laryngoscopes, endotracheal tubes, syringes, needles and the drugs needed for resuscitation were placed on each ward. The nursing staff were instructed in external cardiac massage and the management of cardiac arrests. Doubtless this saved lives.

In 1965, only basic nursing care was offered at the San. A particularly sick patient might have a nurse "special" them, which meant a nurse would look after only that one patient with no other nursing duties. Otherwise, sick patients were transferred by ambulance to the nearest public hospital, either Hornsby Ku-ring-gai District Hospital or the Royal North Shore Hospital. The lack of intensive nursing care severely limited the type of surgery that could be done at the San, meaning only fit patients having relatively minor and routine elective surgery could be operated on.

At this time, an article was published in the *Medical Journal of Australia* from the Royal Melbourne Hospital, describing the establishment of what became known as an Intensive Care Unit (ICU). I visited the Royal Melbourne Hospital's ICU and met the founder and director, who kindly gave me advice on the establishment of an ICU at the San.

It was difficult to locate a suitable site for such a ward in the ageing hospital. The San was still the original wooden building, then more than 60 years old. We combined two adjacent rooms by making a doorway between them, then equipped them appropriately. Our hospital engineer oversaw the building alterations and the installation of piped oxygen and suction. Bedside monitors and the specialised intensive-care beds were purchased. I visited the factory where these beds were manufactured, to make sure that they would meet our needs and would fit through the doorways at the San!

It was clearly necessary to have a suitably trained registered nurse to provide the specialised nursing care required in ICU. The first registered nurse who undertook the specialist training was Jan Fleming, who went to the Royal Melbourne Hospital and completed its ICU training program. Initially there were few patients in the ICU, but when very sick patients were admitted, Jan worked long shifts. Once it became clear to medical staff that the San was capable of caring for these patients, the workload steadily increased and more registered nurses underwent the specialised ICU training.

When plans were being laid to build a new hospital to replace the original wooden structure, medical colleague Dr Russell Butler and I were given the opportunity to develop detailed plans for a new, expanded and modern intensive care unit. We carefully investigated the design parameters of the latest intensive care units, particularly the cabling linking bedside monitors to an elevated central nursing station from which patients could be monitored visually and electronically. Intensive care was to be located on the same floor as the operating theatre and the X-ray department, so critically ill patients could be quickly and safely moved between these departments as needed. This location was also close to the pathology department.

During the construction phase of the new hospital in the early 1970s, it was discovered that the architects had totally enclosed the ICU—along with every other facility on the second floor—without any windows. At the time, there were a number of publications in the medical journals regarding the significant impairment in mental wellbeing of patients who were excluded from sunlight or could not see the natural transitions between day and night. At considerable expense and with great reluctance, the precast concrete panels enclosing the ICU were cut at intervals and windows were installed. This has made a difference for both patients and staff over the years since.

The new intensive care unit proved increasingly important in the development of the San and particularly in the establishment of the open-heart surgery program. Without the ICU, it would have been difficult—perhaps impossible—to establish the highly-specialised cardiac surgery program at the San.

These examples of vision and innovation are some of the many initiatives that improved patient outcomes, increased staff skills and propelled the San to the place where, in the mid-1970s, a comprehensive cardiac surgical service could be contemplated and established. Dr Clifford continues the story:

Early news of the San's intention to start a cardiac surgery program reached the "big end of town"—the prominent surgeons holding a monopoly of that branch of surgery at Sydney's public teaching hospitals. As CEO of the San at the time, I was invited to a meeting of heart surgeons at one of Sydney's major teaching hospitals. They made clear their profound reservations in relation to resources, standards and the viability of a heart surgery program in a private hospital. I was counselled against an attempt to start a heart surgery program at the San, the suggestion being that "it could end in embarrassment to an institution of otherwise high reputation."

As I was leaving the meeting, one of the distinguished surgeons, whom I had not previously met, whispered to me, "Don't worry too much about what was said today."

This was the singular message I took to heart. At the time, I did not disclose to my associates at the San the doubt and fear with which I was confronted at that meeting. It could only have been disconcerting to those who, even at that early stage, were contributing so much toward the endeavour.

The surgeon who whispered the encouragement that meant so much to me was Dr Mark Shanahan, a pioneer of cardiothoracic surgery and heart transplant at St Vincent's Hospital, Sydney. If he had said to me "Fear not", he'd have passed for an angel!

The San's cardiac program had further opposition. New South Wales Health Department administrators—perhaps briefed by interested parties within the public sector—cautioned against the introduction of heart surgery at our hospital.[1] At the same time, it was pointed out that no legal powers existed to prevent the San proceeding. In a courteous response to the Health Department, we conveyed our intention to proceed, giving our best assurances of diligent preparation for the delivery of a service of the quality for which the San had long been known.

An exhaustive planning process for the cardiac program began. This included doctor recruitment, staff training, sourcing specialised equipment, fit-out of cardiac catheterisation labs and a further upgrade to intensive care, as well as extensive nurse education.

The cardiac service at the San was underway—even as opposition continued. A foremost issue was aftercare—what happens to patients in the critical hours and days after heart surgery. The San had long been preparing staff and facilities to address this question. A pilot Intensive Care Unit had been established at the San. Dr Warren Millist (anaesthetist), Dr Russell Butler (physician) and Dr John Grant (neurosurgeon) were its founding consultants. The first ICU managers were Jan Fleming and Tony Hutapea.

As the San's cardiac program grew, Dr Ross Wilson, then Director of the San's Perfusion Service, was instrumental in providing guidance to upgrades of the intensive care and coronary care units. The latter was a new facility for cardiac patients who required continuing high-level care but were not as critical as those needing intensive care. This raised the San's cardiac service to an operation ranking among peers. Under Dr Wilson's guidance and the work of fellow surgeons and nurse leaders Rudi Morgan, Janette Whittaker, John Hodge, Russell Lee and their teams, the San's "aftercare" status became highly regarded.

Dr Wilson also helped guide the San's quality management program at a critical stage of development of the quality initiative at the San, which remains a foundation of excellence in practice today. His uncompromising approach to standards, his command of the health disciplines and generosity in sharing knowledge, as well as his personal qualities of approachability and integrity, made an immeasurable contribution to the modern San and to its mature cardiac program.

In response to pressure from concerned operatives in the public sector, the New South Wales Government determined to regulate the introduction of particular services in private hospitals. Cardiac surgery and radiotherapy—both of which were already established at the San—along with a list of other activities would require Health Department sanction through licensing prior to implementation. The unconcealed aim was to control and limit the spread of these offerings in the private sector.

At the same time, demand was escalating beyond the capacities of the public hospital system, particularly for cardiac surgery. Waiting lists at public hospitals became a matter of community concern, negative press

Medical Influence

and government embarrassment. Extended waiting lists for heart surgery foreshadowed a higher incidence of emergencies, with the prospect of increased morbidity and mortality.

In these circumstances, administrators from Royal North Shore Hospital approached the San to explore the possibility of it taking some private patients on their cardiac surgery waiting lists. It was agreed that the San would accept patients, and that some of Royal North Shore Hospital's cardiologists and cardiac surgeons would be free to apply for San accreditation.

Thus, regulation of the private sector, coupled with escalating demand for services, contributed to the extraordinary growth of the San's cardiac surgery program in the early 1980s. Excellent outcomes were responsible for its success. In a political reversal and with time, the private hospital industry was "deregulated", resulting in the proliferation of cardiac units in New South Wales and other states. The San had shown the way.

By prompting the New South Wales Government to take proscriptive action, then later reversing it, initial opposition to the project can be seen as a significant element in the impact of the San's heart program on the healthcare sector and the community. By extension to a wider range of specialised services which were to follow these first initiatives, the impact has been profound. A later Director-General of Government Regulatory Services was to write:

> Many of these private hospitals now have the capacity to provide a wide range of medical and surgical services which, just a few years ago, were only available within the public hospital sector at the large teaching hospitals.

Another element that unsettled the San's cardiac program near its beginning centred on patient education and rehabilitation. Sharp differences emerged between the San and some doctors regarding the form, potential, implementation and conduct of the cardiac rehabilitation program. Vigorous dialogue over a long period led inevitably to the divisive question of who "owned" the program and the patient.[2] This issue raised the stakes in what threatened to become a self-defeating distraction.

A strong commitment to patient education and cardiac rehabilitation was what had "sold" the cardiac program to a hesitant San Board at the outset. There could be no retreat now. A wholistic approach to healthcare is integral to the philosophy of the Seventh-day Adventist Church and its institutions. Prevention, education and rehabilitation rank with therapy and recovery as parts of this endeavour and are aligned with the San's mission.

The San's cardiac rehabilitation program was designed to promote health and recovery for patients who had experienced a heart attack or major cardiac procedure. The program included dietary adjustment, exercise, counselling and stress management. It encouraged people to make positive lifestyle choices to improve health and reduce the risk of further heart events. This program is stitched into the fabric of the San's mission to care for the body and mind of patients. It helped them to get well and stay well, and to gain confidence in returning to normal life after what—for many—had been a major life-threatening and life-altering experience.

The impact of lifestyle on health and illness is now universally acknowledged. Coronary artery disease presents particular challenges and opportunities for address through prevention, education and rehabilitation.

Medical Influence

A cardiac program without these elements was unthinkable in the setting of an Adventist health service.

When the cardiac rehab program's existence was threatened by consultant disagreement, I took the extraordinary step of seeking legal advice, the only occasion I did so in 23 years of hospital administration. My inquiry was about latitude to revise the contracts with the doctors. Counsel from a senior Sydney lawyer was tangential and unexpected. "Try just dropping the argumentation," he advised. "No more meetings, no more discussion—just go ahead with the program." This worked: tensions declined and the day was saved.

Tens of thousands of patients have benefited physically and psychologically from the San's cardiac diagnostic, medical, surgical and rehabilitation programs over the years. This is testament to many doctors, nurses and other staff at the San who contributed so much.

In the face of many obstacles, the San persisted with its vision of introducing a comprehensive "heart-care" program. Successfully accomplished, its services also brought relief to an overwhelmed public health system. With other developments, a new path was pioneered for the private hospital industry, one that was to propel the San as a leader in healthcare in Australia.

Another example of vision and innovation was the San's first forays into volunteer surgical outreach in developing countries. In 1973, in support of San nurse Lens Larwood and his wife Betty, who were working in the Solomon Islands, a small team from the San travelled to Atoifi Adventist Hospital.

Atoifi Hospital had opened in 1966, but San nurses had been working in medical clinics in the Solomon Islands for a number of decades.

Dr Clifford tells the story of the San's first outreach visits:

> The Atoifi venture was an early trial of a new model of

outreach for the San; a model that included a suitably qualified team visiting—for a defined period—to introduce a new health service or enhance an existing service in developing countries. Emphasis was given to training and enabling local personnel. The provision or upgrading of equipment and facilities was a further objective. Selected Atoifi Hospital staff were also afforded opportunity to travel to Australia for further experience.

For the first visit to Atoifi Hospital in 1973, the San team consisted of Dr Warren Millist (the anaesthetist), nurses Cheryl Borgas and Dawn Maberly, and me (the surgeon). The trip involved a flight via Papua New Guinea, a bumpy overland journey up the western coast of Malaita in an old Rover, followed by an overnight sail in a flat-bottomed launch down the eastern coast of Malaita to Uru Harbour, the home of Atoifi Hospital.

Some 40 operations were performed during this visit, across a wide spectrum of categories. We worked for 12-hour stretches, with only a short lunch break. All patients who came were assisted. Much credit must go to Dr Millist who, in his meticulous way, screened and prepared all patients, conducted their anaesthesia and supervised their post-operative care. Of course, nothing could have been done without the skilled nursing support our San nurses contributed.

A second surgical outreach visit to Atoifi followed in July, 1978, undertaking a similar number of operations. By this time, a small clearing had been prepared, opening the way for aircraft landing. On this visit, nurses Moran Mason and Kim Hopping joined Dr Millist and me. We were fortunate to have found physician Dr Tom Borody visiting Atoifi on his own account. His creative and diagnostic skills were much valued.

An important objective of these surgical outreach trips

was to enhance the capabilities of local staff, including Dr Haynes Posala, hospital director Lens Larwood, theatre supervisor and educator Ian Cameron, and their associates. The San team strove to make each session and each procedure a strong learning experience. Dr Haynes subsequently spent time at the San.

The Atoifi experiences in the 1970s demonstrated these surgical visits were a practical and effective method of outreach that could be beneficial to recipients, often life-changing. It was also rewarding to program participants, relatively inexpensive—relying on donated time and skills—and an opportunity for philanthropy through gifts of means and materials.

A fundamental change has taken place in outreach endeavours over time. While forms and methods may change in response to technical, cultural and political developments, the urge to share knowledge, bring healing and promote welfare remains.

It would be near-impossible to comprehend all the San's surgical outreach endeavours that have proceeded from that time to the present day. Built on the foundations laid during those first two visits to Atoifi Hospital, the San now has a fully fledged coordinated outreach program, which will be discussed in further chapters.

Quality and governance

Quality and governance are important aspects of the hospital's mission in that they help highlight shortcomings and successes, drive continuous improvement, and promote better results for patients. In the following, anaesthetist Dr Millist outlines some of the initiatives introduced at the San during the 1960s to 1980s that were the foundations for many of the quality and governance practices that continue at the San to this day.

In 1965, there was no epidural service for the labour ward at the San. I had been trained in epidurals at the Royal

Women's Hospital in Melbourne by Dr Kevin McCaul. At the time, Dr McCaul was the only anaesthetist in Australia teaching this technique and certainly no-one was doing labour ward epidurals in Sydney. Since obstetricians were not used to epidurals, the take-up of this form of analgesia was very slow.

One of the first patients I was asked to perform an epidural on was the sister of one of the obstetricians at the San. The epidural worked perfectly and other obstetricians slowly began to use this form of analgesia. During this time, Dr John Knight—known publicly as Dr James Wright—was doing TV medical presentations on Channel 9's *Midday Show*. At his request, I gave an epidural anaesthetic to a patient for an "awake caesarean section" by Dr Robert Stocken. Caesarean section under an epidural anaesthetic was an uncommon procedure at the time and aroused a lot of interest. It meant the mother could be awake for the birth and share that moment with the father. Previously that was not possible during caesarean births.

Another new form of pain relief to help mothers during birth was introduced at the San at this time. Inhalational analgesia in the form of a nitrous oxide analgesic began to be used in the labour ward. This was sometimes referred to as "laughing gas", as it successfully reduced pain and helped mothers relax during birth. Nitrous oxide was considered safe to use during labour and gave the mother more control over her own pain relief.

In 1973, it was recognised that the San needed to have an organised structure for its medical staff. Until that time, any registered medical practitioner could admit their patients to the San and undertake surgery, anaesthesia, obstetrics and any other procedure without limitation. The San had no control over who admitted patients and what they did. The San introduced its own by-laws, and doctors who wished to have admitting "privileges"

Medical Influence

had to apply for those privileges and agree to abide by the San's by-laws.

Dr Millist describes that process, and some of the other developments in the area of quality and governance:

> I had been the secretary of the Medical Board of the Hornsby Public Hospital, so I drafted and personally typed the first draft of the San's new by-laws, modelled on the by-laws of the Hornsby Hospital. These by-laws were modified by Dr Clifford and the San Board and ultimately adopted. Some medical practitioners considered this a restriction of freedom of practice and the new by-laws were not universally welcomed. But two highly regarded medical specialists working at the San were the first to sign up to these by-laws and this broke the ice.
>
> At that time, there was no organisation of visiting specialists into specialist divisions who could work as a team, advising the San administration on the purchase of equipment or developments in the various speciality areas such as orthopaedics or cardiology. Individual advice was not always consistent with broader long-term objectives for the speciality as a whole.
>
> The concept of organising the specialist medical staff into their discrete departments—such as the anaesthetic department, the orthopaedic department, and the obstetrics and gynaecology department—was adopted. Each department was to elect a chairman and hold regular meetings to give advice to the hospital on their speciality area. The organisation of the various medical specialities in this way ensured that all members of each speciality group had an equal voice in advising the hospital. At the time, this was novel in a private hospital.
>
> The anaesthetic department was the first speciality area to be organised into a discrete department. The anaesthetists met quarterly to discuss anaesthetic

matters, and organise rosters and operating theatre lists. They also established an emergency on-call roster to ensure an anaesthetist was available around the clock. All anaesthetists accredited at the San were required to participate in the out-of-hours emergency-call roster as a condition of their accreditation. In return, the anaesthetist working in a regular allocated surgical sessions would have priority for other cases booked into that session if the regular surgeon was away. This gave some security of tenure to the anaesthetist in return for participating in the out-of-hours roster.

This new roster system was unique at the time. Prior to this arrangement, an obstetrician or surgeon needing an anaesthetist out of hours would have to beg and plead to get someone to come, wasting valuable time. The proposal for an out-of-hours roster was resented by many anaesthetists who only wanted to give anaesthetics for elective procedures, sometimes even leaving their own regular surgeons to do the best they could to get an anaesthetist out of hours. As the obstetric work at the San developed, it was particularly important to have out-of-hours anaesthetic cover to avoid foetal and maternal deaths because of delay in getting an anaesthetist during emergencies. Without this out-of-hours service, the expansion of the surgical and obstetric service at the hospital would not have been possible.

At the time, there was no formal mechanism by which the San's medical director and hospital management could obtain informed, independent medical advice on how to deal with difficult urgent issues. I proposed to CEO Dr Clifford that a Medical Advisory Committee be established to fill this gap. This proposal was accepted. In subsequent years, a medical advisory committee became a formal part of the administrative structure required by the Australian Hospital Accreditation policy. The San was the first private

Medical Influence

hospital to establish this committee and this model was then adopted by other private hospitals.

Another area to benefit from the guidance and oversight from a diverse group of experts was the operating theatres. Initially the management of operating theatres was essentially the domain of one individual. When the San was rebuilt in the 1970s, six new operating theatres were already in construction when it was noted, by doctors and anaesthetists, that there were design problems with the way the new theatre complex was laid out.

One of the major issues was that the recovery ward was too small and too far away from the theatres. This meant that there was a long journey with a semi-conscious patient without equipment to manage emergencies. To address these issues, the San formed a theatre management committee to ensure that comprehensive, appropriately qualified and informed advice on theatre management was given to the hospital administration. The theatre management committee had input from surgeons, anaesthetists, nursing staff and administration, ensuring a better-run department.

One of the important actions taken by this new committee was to arrange operating lists so that surgeons booked a half- or full-day operating list at appropriate intervals— weekly, fortnightly, monthly—according to their work load, to avoid lists consisting of single cases with different surgeons and anaesthetists for each case. With the way it had been done, if one surgeon or anaesthetist was late, the whole list was disrupted. With different types of surgery, it used to be necessary to set up different types of equipment for each operation, which was inefficient for theatre staff. Booking full operating lists for surgeons in an organised and coordinated way greatly improved the efficiency of surgery.

In 1980, the operating theatres needed major renovation to cope with increased demand and changing technology. As part of this renovation, a dedicated endoscopy theatre was built directly opposite the recovery ward. This theatre quickly became a busy specialised endoscopy theatre. Prior to this time, gastroscopies and colonoscopies were performed without an anaesthetist. The practice was for the endoscopist to administer Pethidine and Valium, then concentrate on the gastroscopy or colonoscopy. I volunteered to provide sedation and, when sometimes necessary, general anaesthesia to facilitate these procedures. This made a significant difference to the ability to conduct a satisfactory examination of the bowel and ensure the safety and comfort of the patient. This practice of having an anaesthetist in attendance during endoscopies and colonoscopies was soon made a hospital requirement and standard practice.

In the early 1980s, the Director of Nursing Rose-Marie Radley and I were asked by the San to visit a number of hospitals in the United States to look particularly at day surgery programs and open-heart surgery programs. One of the hospitals we visited was the Kettering Hospital in Dayton, Ohio. While there, we saw the hospital's networked computer system and the enormous efficiencies it brought to hospital management. We were shown how each patient was given a barcode and, as they went through the operating rooms, barcodes from all disposables were added to their records along with barcoded records of surgical procedures and medicines. We were shown how the next morning all of these records were scanned into the hospital's computer, which then generated new orders for replacement stock, prostheses, medicines and pathology requirements. This was also linked to the hospital's accounting system, so an accurate up-to-date statement of account was available at all times.

Medical Influence

This only took about half an hour each morning to record all the data from the previous day's surgery.

On our return to Sydney, we discussed with CEO Dr Clifford the merits of installing such a system at the San. The benefits were obvious compared with the time-consuming method of manually entering data in the theatre records—the norm at the San at that time. This proposal was accepted and, the following year, two young American computer experts came to the San to assist with setting up the San's first integrated computer system.

Not only was this a first for the San but I believe it was the first for any Sydney hospital and perhaps the first for any private hospital in Australia. The networked computer system enabled doctors to instantly and securely access patients' pathology results, X-ray results and medication records from any computer terminal within the hospital. At the time, this was revolutionary. It was not long before the system had to be upgraded, but this was the beginning.

In the mid-1980s, when patient-controlled analgesia was discussed in the anaesthetic literature, I was fortunate to have a medical student allocated to me for an anaesthetic term. At the same time, one of the medical equipment companies provided a patient-controlled analgesia (PCA) machine on a trial basis. A PCA machine administers narcotic pain relief to patients via a drip, and the patient pressed a button that administered a measured dose of narcotic—within limits—whenever they were in pain. This enabled the patient to safely control their own pain. The medical student working with me was required to undertake a project and to write a report on it as part of training requirements, so I asked her to introduce the patient-controlled analgesia machine to the ward. This was a new concept and was a great concern to the nursing staff, who were fearful of patients being allowed to self-administer narcotics. However, this pilot trial proved successful and the increasing literature demonstrated the benefits of patient-controlled analgesia. The San then bought about 15 PCA machines and protocols were drawn up to safeguard their use. This marked the beginning of an acute pain management service at the San.

Ethics and excellence

In the 1970s, Dr Clifford saw much potential in the emerging field of ethics to inform healthcare decision-making and promote better outcomes for patients. The following is his account of the history of ethics at the San:

> Little more than half a century ago, ethics as a discipline—if featured at all in schools of learning—was buried within other offerings such as philosophy. Some older religious traditions have a history of scholarship in the field, but focus on the study of ethics has not been a strength within the broadly evangelical movement. This reality was brought home to me when a one-time chairman of the San's Board questioned the need for "the spending of time and resources on ethics" at the San. Behind these reservations was doubtless the conviction that the teachings of church doctrine provide sufficient guidance on moral questions. At worst, some saw the teaching of ethics as a challenge to religious instruction.[3]

> The principles embodied in the biblical narrative do offer a rich and invaluable source of moral guidance.[4] But issues are not addressed in detail, nor many of the questions raised by advancing technologies. This is where the gift of moral agency enters. Ethics as a discipline is simply human moral agency at work.

> One outcome arising out of the application of new technologies is that society is confronted by questions never previously asked. The life sciences have experienced a foremost impact. In healthcare, a large

Medical Influence

component of ethics has to do with beginning-of-life and end-of-life questions, and with the application of reproductive and genetic technologies. Currently, there is little in the broad field of health enterprise that has not been addressed from the ethical perspective; from research to carer–patient relationships, from organ transplantation to genetic manipulation and patient rights.

In the belief that Adventist Christian heritage had much to contribute to the debate on questions touching human life, the San took an early interest in issues in the collective category of "Bioethics". Its first initiatives—in the 1970s—were humble. At my request, then-School of Nursing administrative assistant, Jenny Baldwin collected newspaper clippings on ethical topics in the health field; there was a surprising volume. These clippings were employed to demonstrate a growing public interest in ethics; something to which the San, the Church and its institutions would need to respond. This unique collection, the first building block of a comprehensive ethics library, is instructive to browse even today.

In 1978, the San's ethics program received much impetus from the visit of Jack Provonsha, Emeritus Professor of Christian Ethics and Founding Director of the Center for Christian Bioethics at Loma Linda University, California. A distinguished academic, he had pioneered a place for the study of Applied Ethics at that institution.

So enthusiastic was the response to Professor Provonsha's presentations at the San that the carefully planned speaking schedule had to be expanded. Often it was "standing room only" at his talks, as word filtered out and community members joined staff for his lectures. Such was the level of interest, the hospital launched a "brown bag" lunch initiative, in which staff could take a packed lunch to eat while listening to the professor's lectures during their meal breaks.

The San held 11 bioethics conferences between 1986 and 1998. The information from these conferences was compiled in journal form and made available to attendees. These records can be accessed from the San Library. The ethics conferences were an outstanding mission initiative and an important part of Christian outreach.

While the San owned a comprehensive clinical library, its ethics resources had also built up considerably over the years. Bioethics source material had advanced from newspaper clippings to a substantial library of reference volumes. Literature in the field was multiplying at a pace in keeping with global interest in the new discipline. The decision to establish a Bioethics Library as a distinct unit within the San Library accomplished several things: it afforded a readily available source of reference for staff, students and educators; it opened the way for further study in the discipline; and it provided sources for the hospital's Research Committee.

The Bioethics Library was also accessible to members of other institutions and the interested public. With more than 8000 volumes and many subscription journals, it has become one of the larger Bioethics collections in Australia. A former hospital chaplain and one-time Director of the Christian Centre for Bioethics, Dr Tom Ludowici was instrumental in the development of the Bioethics Library to this status. The facility has been named for him.

At the beginning of the ethics enterprise, the San was involved in only occasional research activity, mainly associated with the pursuit of higher qualifications by staff. When an Ethics Committee was established in 1988, its work was expected to lie largely in the field of policy development and the resolution of clinical problems. However, associated with its rebuilding and entry into higher-speciality fields, the ascendancy of the hospital attracted an increasing number of consultants with teaching affiliations. The San came to be seen as a potential base for participation in research. At the same time, in response to the "ethics demand" and acting on Commonwealth government authority, the National Health and Medical Research Council (NHMRC) established a comprehensive nation-wide program of research governance. Every human research proposal required review, endorsement and monitoring by a duly appointed institutional human-research ethics committee. The San's Ethics Committee was ready-formed, requiring only a little adjustment to conform to regulator standards.

Today, the San has an NHMRC-accredited Human Research Ethics Committee, which considers all research proposals at the hospital. Some projects are generated within the hospital, others are multicentred, with the San participating in both national and international research arenas. More recently, the Australasian Research Institute has been established, based at the San, with the hospital's Human Research Ethics Committee acting as its referral body for review.

The overriding concern of the Ethics Committee is the wellbeing and safety of people who participate in research projects, predominantly patients under the San's care. Other important contributions the Ethics Committee make include:

- Ensuring the worthiness of research projects.
- Offering advice and assurance to the researcher.
- Protecting the interests and standing of the hospital.
- Supporting the worldwide human research endeavour and its goals.

"Take Me to the Sun"

Ethics initiatives at the San have travelled a long and interesting road since the 1970s. The San today is immeasurably richer and its processes more rigorous as a result. More than five decades of ethics focus and expertise has contributed to excellence in standards, decision-making and care.

1. Reasons that were given for regulation—and thus limiting—of the offerings of speciality services in private hospitals included:
    - Insufficiency of resource and experience to vouch safe outcome in private hospitals.
    - The exercise of "case selectivity" by private hospitals, resulting in a disproportionate burden of care and cost-intensive cases devolving on the public sector.
    - Compromise of teaching standards in public hospitals through distortion of caseload.
    - The inroad and impact of new dimensions of entrepreneurship in the health industry.
    - Imposition on health funding arrangements between the public and private sectors and between Commonwealth and State governments.

    There can be no question also that a certain "territorialism" prevailed, protective of the interests of operatives and units in established public centres. In many cases, doctors and specialists would understandably have direct or indirect material interest in protecting their patient-referral base. Today, many senior doctors in the larger public teaching hospitals also enjoy operating privileges in private hospitals. Affiliations between public and private hospitals are not uncommon, and private units have been built in juxtaposition to their public counterparts.

2. The "ownership" issue: An older hierarchical model of patient–doctor–hospital relationships sees the patient as "belonging" to the doctor, with the hospital providing accommodation and certain services to the doctor and, through him or her, to the patient. In the contemporary dynamic, the patient engages providers for particular services. This places providers in a lateral relationship of cooperation and partnership. Hospitals offer doctors certain privileges of facility and access, and doctors serve the hospital and patients through the provision of clinical skills and services. When the hospital "privileges" system was introduced, some doctors found it uncongenial and even threatened lawsuit. The latter never materialised. The new dynamic is protective of, and in the interests of, all parties.

3. The New South Wales Schools Ethics/Religious class debate has been ongoing for several years. Strong views are held on both sides.

4. Scripture affords a mandate for ethics as a study (see, for example, 1 Thessalonians 5:21). A vast resource of literature has now accumulated on Theological Perspectives on Bioethical issues. A definitive anthology is the volume *On Moral Medicine*, Third Edition, Eerdmans, 2012.

Nursing Influence

Dr Alex S Currie, Dr Alan Gibbons and Annette Baldwin

Since the San opened its doors to the public in January, 1903, it has been a change agent in the healthcare industry in many ways. As we have seen in previous chapters, the San has continued to pioneer new technologies, and establish facilities and services ahead of its contemporaries in many instances. The San has not done this for innovation's sake, but to keep its mission commitment to care for the body, mind and spirit of those it serves—in the best way it can.

In a similar spirit, San nurses have been influential, not only in the care of patients but in shaping nursing culture in Australia, as well as impacting generations of people in the South Pacific and beyond. The following illustrates ways the San has fostered nursing leaders and how San nurses have always been an integral expression of the San's core mission.

Australia's first male nurses

While much has been said in recent times about gender inequality in the workforce, what is less known is that as recently as the 1970s, one sector of the Australian workforce was entirely female-dominated. For the first two-thirds of the 20th century, men weren't welcome in the nursing workforce in hospitals throughout Australia. But the San bucked this trend.

The first male nurses to graduate in Australia were trained at the

San. The hospital began training male nurses as soon as it opened in 1903, while throughout the rest of Australia male nurses were not accepted until many decades later. Because Australia was a British colony, it adopted nursing practices from the "mother country", influenced largely by Florence Nightingale, whose philosophies led to the demise of men from this caring profession. However, because the San's first health administrators came from United States, they brought with them American medical practices and nursing standards. This became a notable cross-cultural influence and, under the American model, the San accepted both men and women into nurse training. In this way, the San's nursing culture was decades ahead of its time and the San's male-nurse training program eventually helped change and shape the broader Australian nursing culture.

Because the San educated male nurses, and taught and practised massage and hydrotherapy, the British Medical Association blacklisted the San until 1912. Nurse training in general at the San was not recognised by the New South Wales Government until 1927, and male nurses were not recognised by the State for more than 60 years after the San trained and employed its first male nurses.

> Entry into schools of nursing was dependent on gaining the approval of the matron and it would appear that, in metropolitan Sydney at least, this was difficult to obtain. For example, at the Royal Prince Alfred Hospital (RPA) in 1950, despite a shortage of nursing tutors, the application of two qualified tutors—a married couple from England—was rejected because the board was not prepared to employ a man. The first male nurse was not employed at RPA until 1966, when Lance Waddington (San graduate, 1949) was appointed. It was a further three years before a man was accepted for general training at RPA and it was not until the 1970s that men were accepted for training at St Vincent's Hospital (1972) and Manly Hospital (1975).[1]

Nursing Influence

The inclusion of men in the hospital's workforce made a difference in many ways. For male patients uncomfortable being nursed by women, males brought confidence and a sense of comfort. Men also brought different skills and strengths to nursing, complementing those of women. And for men who wanted to work in the caring profession of nursing, they had the opportunity to do so at the San without discrimination because of their gender.

Broader nursing influence

During nurse training at the San, many students were invited to preach in churches across Sydney. This practice was particularly prevalent in the early-to-mid 1900s and was an extension of the San's mission to care for the spirit, not only the spiritual needs of patients at the San but of people in the broader community. After completing nurse training, some nurses studied further and became ministers of religion, using this combined skill set for valuable ministry.

In the following, retired San chaplain Dr Alex Currie recalls the stories of several men who trained as male nurses at the San and went on to become preachers:

> Edmund Rudge enrolled at the San in 1904. After nurse training, Rudge held the position of head male nurse at the San before moving to other roles and becoming a minister in 1916. For the next four decades, he served in senior leadership positions in the Seventh-day Adventist Church throughout Australia, as well as Fiji, Britain and northern Europe.
>
> Claude Judd is another San-trained nurse, who entwined nurse education with theological education. The Judd family lived on an isolated family farm near Drouin, Victoria, in the 1930s. Claude earnestly desired to train as a minister at the Australasian Missionary College, but did not have enough money for college fees. A San nursing graduate of 1926, Max Grolimund, who became a minister

of religion, was their district pastor. Pastor Grolimund visited Claude and suggested he enrol at the San to study nursing. That way he could earn money while nursing to help pay for further education as a minister, if that's what he wished.

Claude began nurse training at the San in 1938. During his time at the San, one of the chaplains periodically conducted suburban evangelistic series and Claude helped out as an usher. "That's how I became interested in pastoral evangelism," Claude explained. He and some of his colleagues were occasionally asked to conduct church services in some of the smaller churches around Sydney. "Those of us who were willing were placed on the preaching roster, and the San paid our bus and train fares," Claude said. "We went as far as Lithgow [to preach], which meant an all-day trip."

Claude graduated from nursing at the San in 1941. He discovered he had an affinity for preaching and ministering to others, and went on to work in ministry for more than 30 years at local, state and national levels. The San presented a special citation to Claude during the hospital's Homecoming celebrations in August, 2016. For Claude, the San experience—the way he was treated and what he was taught—influenced his life and shaped his ministry. In turn, he served many others, both as a nurse and as a pastor.

Allan Wilby Tilley of Mount Gambier, South Australia, completed a year of biblical studies at the Australasian Missionary College before enrolling in the San's general nursing course in the early 1940s. When Allan graduated from the San in 1943, he spent a couple of years as a ministerial intern in places like Glen Innes, Tenterfield and Moree (New South Wales) before marrying fellow nurse, Ruth Pretyman, in 1945. Together they sailed to

Nursing Influence

Papua New Guinea as missionary nurses a month after their wedding. The ship dropped them off on a beach near Aroma—in the south-eastern region of Papua New Guinea—to provide healthcare and serve the local community. In 1948, they were invited to relocate to Kwalabesi on the island of Malaita (Solomon Islands) to manage a medical clinic and oversee the mission station. In 1956, Allan commenced work in the San's pathology department until his retirement in 1978.

This is only a sample of the many San nurses who added ministry to their nursing qualification. At least 40 male graduates from the San went on to train as ministers of religion. The San produced graduates who were competent, compassionate, caring and practical. Because of the San's hospital-based training at that time, its graduates spent much time on the wards with patients and they tended to be down-to-earth, personable, conversational and approachable. The San had a strong influence in moulding their lives, and graduates became living examples of "Christianity in Action" in Australia and overseas.

Dr Currie recalls working in New Britain—an island between Papua New Guinea and the Solomon Islands—in the late 1960s, where he helped establish a tertiary college. His story illustrates how the San's influence reaches unexpected places:

> In 1968, while helping establish Sonoma College, New Britain, I needed large bamboo to build a temporary residence for young ladies who were to be enrolled in the college. At the time, my wife was teaching two young children of a cocoa plantation owner called Don Dunbar-Reid. I told Don of our need and asked him where we might source enough bamboo for the girls' dormitory. He suggested I visit Vimy Plantation and ask the owner, Mr Joycey, if the college could harvest bamboo from his property. But Don informed me that

"Take Me to the San"

Mr Joycey, who had lost an eye on the battlefields of France, could be a challenging character with whom to interact.

I drove to Vimy Plantation in the college's three-ton Toyota truck, parked it outside the Joycey residence and knocked on the front door of Mr Joycey's house. An elderly man came to the screen door, didn't open it, and said fairly gruffly, "What do you want?" I was taken aback by this abrupt beginning but explained that I was a new neighbour and wanted to meet them. "But what do you want?" he asked again. I informed him through the closed screen door that the Seventh-day Adventist Church had purchased an old plantation nearby, and was establishing a tertiary training college to educate teachers, secretaries, accountants, ministers, builders and agriculturists. Mr Joycey opened the screen door and abruptly pointed to chairs and a table on the verandah and said, "Sit down".

He called his wife, saying, "This man represents those angels." I didn't know what he meant by that. But he explained that he'd been a patient at the San many years previously, near the end of the war, and that he and his wife were familiar with the institution and its link to Seventh-day Adventists. From what I understood, one of their children had also been born at the San. From their experience at the San, they likened the nurses to "angels". Because of that link to the San years earlier, and the impact the organisation and its people had on him and his family, Mr Joycey provided all the bamboo required for the girls' dormitory at Sonoma College—in a country thousands of kilometres from the San.

Stories such as these illustrate the San and its nurses have been influential far beyond the hospital itself. As San staff go about their day-to-day work living out the San's mission, they might not stop to

Nursing Influence

think what possible impacts their ministry has on people's lives in the broader community and further afield.

San nurses in the South Pacific

Throughout the past century, San nurses travelled, worked and lived all over the globe. One area where the impact of San nurses has been particularly evident is in the South Pacific. It is impossible to list all the people in all the roles in all the places in the world where San nurses have made a difference. Many islands in the South Pacific benefited because of work San nurses did in healthcare, education and ministry. Dr Currie recounts a few examples:

> In the 1890s, a successful trader and plantation owner, Norman Wheatley, lived and built his empire in the western Solomon Islands. Mr Wheatley owned several ships, both sailing ships and motorised ships, and frequently travelled to Sydney for stores, equipment and medical attention. According to his family, he was a patient at the San on several occasions between 1912 and 1914, receiving treatment for illnesses such as malaria. The magazine *Life and Health* was posted regularly from Australia to traders, government officials and expatriates living in the Solomons, and perhaps Wheatley first read about the San in that magazine. While a patient in the San, Wheatley was most impressed with the treatment, care and compassion of the medical staff. He enjoyed hearing staff singing during chapel services and the peaceful, harmonious atmosphere it brought to the hospital. He also appreciated the cleanliness of the hospital and its health message—a message unique at the time as it encouraged good nutrition, exercise, trust in God, sunshine and fresh air, natural remedies, hydrotherapy, massage and temperance, including avoiding tobacco and alcohol. There is evidence in historical documents that Wheatley spoke to the then-president of the Seventh-day Adventist Church about

whether Adventists would consider working in the Solomon Islands to establish health and education services where there were none. Perhaps that is why the Adventist church decided to build a ship, the *Advent Herald*, for use in mission work in the Solomon Islands and Pacific region.

Around the same time that Wheatley was in and out of the San as a patient, a man called Griffiths F Jones served as a chaplain at the San (1913–14). Jones was a former Welsh sea captain who at the age of 26 had gained a Master Mariner's certificate in Liverpool, England, in 1890. While chaplain at the San, it appears Jones became acquainted with Wheatley. Out of that friendship between the two men came the idea that if Jones sailed a ship to the western Solomon Islands to commence mission activities there—because of the respect he had for both Jones and the San—Wheatley would provide a temporary crew for the ship. Jones agreed.

On Wheatley's return to the western Solomon Islands early in 1914, he kept his word. He summoned his employees together, informing them a new Christian mission was coming and, wherever he travelled on his ship throughout the Solomons, Wheatley broadcast this news. He is reported to have taken a wind-up gramophone with a big speaker to Viru Harbour and played a recording of people singing, telling them the new mission would teach them to sing like he heard staff singing at the San.

Jones and his wife Marion made preparations for this new endeavour and set sail for the Solomon Islands. They arrived in May, 1914, where they met up again with Wheatley. He provided them with a small crew for the ship and gave them "good advice" about life in

Nursing Influence

their new country. Jones and his wife slept on the floor of one of Wheatley's stores in Viru Harbour until their small two-bedroom house was built. To a large degree, this exciting pioneering venture was influenced by relationships established at the San between Jones and Wheatley.

Within weeks, Jones recognised the great medical needs in the Solomons and requested help from Australia. A young couple from the San, Oscar Hellestrand and Ella Sharp—daughter of Pastor Frederick Sharp, who was a member of the first search group in 1899 to view the land that was eventually chosen to build the San—stepped up to the challenge. In 1915, as a newly-married couple, they accepted the invitation to provide medical services for the church in the Solomon Islands. They sailed from Sydney to the western Solomon Islands and Viru Harbour became their home.

There were no hospitals to which they could send patients. Typically, the Hellestrands treated malaria, ringworm, yaws and hookworm, and dressed wounds from accidents. A local chief by the name of Pana, visited them every day for treatment to a leg ulcer. While they treated him, this local leader taught the Hellestrands the local language, which they learned quickly. Besides providing a great deal of medical procedures, the Hellestrands conducted a school for about 50 students, teaching English, Bible, music and simple home remedies, even though they were not trained teachers. Two years later, with Oscar suffering from malaria and the birth of their first child imminent, the Hellestrands decided to return to Australia.

Because of families such as the Jones and the Hellestrands who left the San and served as early pioneer medical missionaries in the Solomon Islands, many nurses have followed their example. Three nurses died while working there: Muriel Parker in 1930, Brian Dunn in 1965 and Lens Larwood in 1979. Many San-trained staff continued that pioneering work throughout the past century, establishing health clinics, schools and hospitals. As a result, close to 1000 Solomon Island nurses, doctors, pastors, teachers, accountants and office workers have travelled from the Solomons to establish services in other countries such as Papua New Guinea. So San nurses have enjoyed an ongoing influence throughout the Pacific Islands.

The difference one nurse can make

San nurses do not have to go overseas to make a difference. Many nurses have left their mark on the San and advanced the nursing profession.

Since the San was established, quality nursing care has been one of the principal goals of the institution. The person primarily responsible for the calibre of nurses and nursing care was the matron. Historically, matrons at the San were appointed on the basis of their former nursing experience, as well as their personal and professional attitudes and values. Most matron appointees came to their positions with natural leadership and management talents, and were considered skilful and competent nurses.

Traditionally, the matron—the most senior nurse—was responsible for establishing and maintaining the desired standard for quality nursing care practiced within the institution. Matrons also assumed other roles, including the management of food service, controlling laundry services, directing the cleaning staff, supervising the nurses' residence, and co-ordinating and teaching in the nurse-training program. The San had a number of great matrons over the years. The longest-serving was Rose-Marie Radley, who served 23 years.

Dr Alan Gibbons—a San nursing graduate of 1960, who held a number of management and nurse-educator roles at the San for 20

Nursing Influence

years—reflects on the many ways one person, living out the San's mission, could make a difference to patients, staff, the hospital and the nursing profession:

> Miss Radley graduated from the San in 1953 and undertook extensive post-registration experience, including working in public and private hospitals in New South Wales before travelling overseas to work in Canada, Taiwan and Hong Kong. She held the positions of matron in both Taiwan and Hong Kong Adventist Hospitals, and her experience included the commissioning of the new Hong Kong Adventist Hospital.
>
> Among her post-registration qualifications, she completed a Midwifery Certificate and a Diploma in Nursing Administration. Miss Radley returned to the San in 1972, initially as Deputy Matron. She was the first nurse administrator employed at the San with a tertiary qualification in Nursing Administration. In 1972, a year after her return to the San, she was promoted to Matron, and her title was changed the following year to Director of Nursing—a role she held until 1996. This was the beginning of a new era for nursing at the San.
>
> Miss Radley adopted an eclectic leadership style. She particularly encouraged her staff to work as team members, and implemented processes to reduce complaints and possible injuries to staff and patients. In line with her proactive philosophy, she encouraged nursing managers and administrators to conduct regular ward rounds to identify patient-care issues before they developed into major problems.
>
> Miss Radley was a visionary leader, being very aware that even the smallest nursing activity impacted not only on the patients themselves but on the outcomes of the hospital's service as a whole. She recognised the importance of the

San's mission and viewed nursing care to be wholistic in nature.

She led her employees to develop as professionals and undertake further study, especially for those working in new specialist areas. She also delegated to carefully selected staff members the responsibilities of conducting evaluative trials of new treatments and equipment.

She had a strong faith and trust in God and believed in the power of prayer, regularly seeking God's assistance and guidance in her work. She encouraged her staff to pray at the beginning of their work shifts each day.

Consistent with her philosophy of working in teams and continually striving for excellence, she brought staff together from nursing administration, the various wards and nursing education, establishing numerous committees. These committees included Quality Management, Infection Control, Wound Management, Budgeting, Accreditation and School of Nursing.

Miss Radley also encouraged her nursing staff to research aspects of contemporary nursing practice. One example of this was when she led her nursing team to develop a philosophy of nursing supporting a wholistic approach, delivering nursing care in a way that met patient's physical, mental, social and spiritual needs. She also led the change in the delivery of nursing from "job assignment" to "team nursing", and worked with her staff to revolutionise patient charts, including developing a new medication chart, nursing history chart, nursing care plan and a neurological assessment chart.

During Miss Radley's leadership at the San, she helped facilitate the development of new and improved clinical nursing areas within the hospital. Radley was part of the frontline teams involved in initiatives such as commissioning an angiography laboratory; the implementation of the cardiac surgery program; rebuilding the intensive care unit; and the commissioning of a coronary care unit, emergency unit and a day surgery unit. She also oversaw the redevelopment of the maternity unit, operating theatres and recovery, and the commissioning of a renal dialysis unit, a paediatric sleep centre and the rebuilding of the School of Nursing.

Miss Radley also committed to upgrading the nursing profession and thereby enhanced the quality of nursing care practiced at the hospital and beyond. She made a significant contribution to nursing education by promoting and facilitating the transfer of the hospital-based nurse-training program to a tertiary-level program. This was one of the significant outcomes of her tenure as a leader of the San. Dr Gibbons outlines how this process was undertaken:

> During the late 1960s to early 1970s, there was a strong movement by the nursing profession in Australia and overseas, to improve the standard of nurse training and, by extension, improve the standard of care for patients.

Following multiple studies into nursing education broadly throughout New South Wales, it was recommended that:

- The New South Wales Nurses Registration Board extend the hospital-based nursing syllabus to 1000 theory hours.
- The four-year course be reduced to three years.
- A New South Wales Nurses Education Board be established. The purpose of this new organisation was to:
    1. Further research aspects of nursing education.
    2. Advise the Government of desirable objectives for nursing education.

3. Recommend ways of achieving the proposed stated objectives and to guide educational activities in nursing curricula development.[2]

Nurse training had always been an integral part of the service and mission of the San, traditionally delivered as a hospital-based apprenticeship program. Under Miss Radley's leadership, the San administration, the Nursing Department and the School of Nursing worked together to implement the new statutory requirements for nurse training mandated by the New South Wales Nurses Registration Board. Such requirements included increased teaching hours of obligatory subject themes and specified hours in particular areas of clinical nursing practice.

Rapid developments in scientific and medical technology, together with changes in society and education, brought about new approaches to the way healthcare was delivered. This necessitated a complete appraisal of nursing education and the delivery of nursing practice. As a result, there was a perceived need to transfer nursing education to the tertiary sector of education, in line with what was underway in Canada, the United States, England, Scotland and New Zealand.

The earlier nurse-education approaches used in the hospital-based apprenticeship system in Australia had frequently been portrayed as a "second-rate" nurse-training system. It was described as detrimental to the professional development of the registered nurse, compared with the educational approaches used for the education of other members of the medical and paramedical health team. There was increasing agitation by the Australian nursing profession for nurse training to be moved from the hospital-based system to the college and university systems.

Nursing Influence

This was in line with the trend throughout developed countries for the nursing profession to have a higher education pre-entry standard as well as a more scientifically oriented training program.

In a similar vein, the World Health Organization noted that because nurses were expected to provide the most skilled nursing care in hospitals, undertake leadership roles and work in partnership with physicians, it was recommended they be trained in an education setting where the knowledge, skills and attitudes essential for fulfilling these functions could best be acquired.

As Director of Nursing at the San, Miss Radley was insistent that the San's School of Nursing take on the challenge to upgrade and professionalise nurse training. Over a number of years, Mima Burgher and Dr Gibbons shared this task. A nursing curriculum planning group was established to work on the development of a new diploma-level nursing curriculum. Dr Gibbons describes this process:

> We assembled a group of lecturers, academics, registered nurses and student nurses to work on transferring the hospital apprenticeship certificate course to a college tertiary nursing education diploma program. It was the beginning of the San developing and implementing highly respected professional nursing programs in conjunction with its affiliated tertiary institution, Avondale College of Higher Education.

Mission underpinned the development of the new nursing course, making sure the way nurses were trained aligned with the San's ethos. A summary of the San's School of Nursing's philosophy in the proposed new curriculum was stated as:

> Nursing is an art and a science involving the total patient; promoting spiritual, psychological and physical health; stressing health education and

preservation; ministering to the sick; caring for the patient's environment; giving health service to the family, in the community and to the individual.[3]

It took a number of years for the new nursing curriculum to be developed and refined, through a number of iterations. The design of the new curriculum followed the pattern of an academic semester with supervised sessions of clinical experience each week, followed by a semester of semi-supervised clinical workforce experience. Throughout the course, a logical sequence was developed to lead the student through a related theoretical and clinical program.

Clinical experience was seen as a vital part of the educational process. The practicums in nursing were planned so students would rotate through periods of clinical nursing on the wards, following a theory semester of learning about a related clinical nursing area. That way, the student would be introduced in-depth to a specific clinical practice field.

The course was accredited by the new Higher Education Board and the New South Wales Nurses Registration Board. The first cohort of students commenced the course in July, 1980. This tertiary-level nursing course was the third in New South Wales and the seventh in Australia.

San nurses have always been taught the integration of the body, mind and spirit—one domain affects the other. The San and the nurse training underwent significant changes during the years Miss Radley was Director of Nursing. The San's mission shaped the initiatives Miss Radley instigated at the San during her tenure. She was a nurse leader who lived mission, promoted and encouraged mission, and put people and processes in place to fulfil mission. Positives have continued to flow from these initiatives in the decades since, resulting in nursing training that is professionally rewarding for nurses, focused on quality patient care and staff development. Aligning nurse training and service delivery with San's mission contributed to the hospital's reputation as a place for high standards and quality nurse training, developing nurses who are highly respected and sought after throughout the healthcare sector.

That commitment to training health professionals continues to this day, as a crucial part of the San's mission. In 2013, the San opened a new Clinical Education Centre onsite, to train nurses, doctors and allied-health professionals. This centre was the first fully-fledged private hospital clinical school in New South Wales. It was possible with collaboration from Adventist HealthCare, the University of Sydney, Avondale College of Higher Education, Health Workforce Australia, the New South Wales State Government and private philanthropy.

The Clinical Education Centre provides unique side-by-side training of different groups of health professionals, including clinical placements for doctors, nurses, physiotherapy, pharmacy, radiography, occupational therapy, orthoptics, midwifery and dietetics.

The centre contains auditoria, clinical skills laboratories, a medical library, tutorial rooms, problem-based learning rooms and lecture rooms. It also has a simulation centre where trainees can experience "live" medical training scenarios. High-tech dummies are able to simulate giving birth, cardiac arrests, having a stroke and other emergency scenarios, thereby honing the skills of trainees before they work in the clinical environment.

In keeping with its mission and belief that good training enhances patient care and leads to better outcomes for patients, each year the Clinical Education Centre provides training for approximately 120 nurses, 30 doctors, and close to 3000 training days for allied-health professionals.

Nursing influence around the world

One would expect the San to care for people within its local community and Sydney more broadly. And it does—more than 186,000 patients come to the San each year. What is less known

"Take Me to the San"

is that since the hospital opened, it has continued to find ways to support people in need across the globe, including places in the South Pacific region, Nepal, India, Mongolia, Myanmar (Burma), Vietnam, Cambodia, Rwanda and Bolivia.

For a private, not-for-profit Christian hospital, the San's influence spread near and far through its graduates and dedicated doctors working in many parts of the world. As mentioned in the previous chapter, nurses were part of the first surgical outreach trips in the 1970s when a small team visited Atoifi Adventist Hospital in the Solomon Islands.

These successful surgical visits to Atoifi laid the foundations for the launch of a dedicated new service. In 1983, Russell Lee, an intensive-care nurse at the San, visited Tonga and saw the need for cardiac surgery in that small island nation. In those days, Tonga had a high incidence of rheumatic fever. This condition left people with rheumatic heart disease, which had devastating effects on the heart valves and function. When Russell returned to Australia, he reported this to his colleagues and doctors at the San. A plan was formulated to do something about it—and "Operation Open Heart" to Tonga was born.

The first team of 45 people—nurses, surgeons and support staff, the majority of them from the San—travelled to Tonga in 1986 to screen patients, perform heart surgery and run health-education programs.

In the years since, the San's Operation Open Heart—later renamed Open Heart International (OHI)—conducted surgical outreach trips to 16 countries and has provided more than 6000 patients with free, life-changing surgery. Some 15 to 20 tonnes of medical equipment is freighted around the world each year to support these medical outreach trips. Importantly, each team now trains doctors and nurses in the countries they visit, with the aim that these countries may gain self-sufficiency in the future.

The San's Open Heart International (OHI) teams have shared many stories about their experiences working on these overseas surgical trips over the years. The first is from Dr Currie:

Nursing Influence

Although Fiji is a wonderful tourist destination, more than a quarter of the population live below the national poverty line. Our family lived in Fiji for five years and made many friends among Fijian and Indian people. One close Indian friend, who tailored uniforms for Fulton College where I was principal at the time, contacted me, advising that his wife had a serious heart condition and could die within a year. Shortly after this, the San's OHI team arrived in Fiji on one of its annual heart surgery trips. Team member Dr Alan Gale agreed to operate on this woman. When she was on the operating table, it was discovered she had an aortic dissection which demanded complex surgery. Had Dr Gale known the extent of her health problem, he might not have operated, but she walked out of hospital a new woman with renewed confidence and is still living more than 20 years later.

At the time, an Australian journalist added to this story under the title "Healing the hearts: Australians working in the Pacific and South-East Asia provide aid that goes way beyond diplomacy":

> Somewhere in Dr Alan Gale's Sydney wardrobe hangs a lime-green crimplene suit. Next to it is a sky-blue silk version and a dark blue pinstripe. For five years, on Gale's annual visits to Fiji's Colonial War Memorial Hospital, an Indian tailor has been sewing suits and shirts in a heartfelt gesture of thanks.
>
> Gale and a team of Australian specialists and nurses saved the life of the tailor's wife six years ago. She was 30 then, and the operation was supposed to be simple, but it became an epic five-hour effort as the team corrected an aortic dissection, a procedure that not only replaces heart valves but the whole arch of the aorta—the major

"Take Me to the San"

artery of the heart responsible for circulating blood around the body.

"Every year he brings her in. . . . They come in every year (to visit us). It's just one example of the gratitude of the recipients," says Gale.

A cardiothoracic surgeon at Sydney Adventist Hospital (the San), Gale has just returned from his 13th trip to Fiji, performing open-heart surgery on 30 patients with a Melbourne paediatric cardiac surgeon, Dr Andrew Cochrane.

With 46 other Australian and New Zealand medical and health professional volunteers, the surgeons have completed the latest trip as part of [Open Heart International], a project coordinated by the San in conjunction with the Adventist Development and Relief Agency and the Australian Agency for International Development. . . .

This year, as is tradition the team was feted with functions, including a dinner and tribal fire-walking demonstration. "At the farewell dinner, when they sing Isa Lei, the Fijian farewell song, it brings tears to my eyes every time I hear it," says Gale.

It is these occasions, he believes—and the smile of a previously ill patient, the soft "thank you", the genuine hugs of appreciation, and the friendships formed between team members and local staff—that make the exhausting two-week, 24-hour-a-day program so worthwhile. And the suits hanging in his wardrobe—priceless.[4]

The Open Heart International volunteer surgical teams operate in many places around the world. A member and coordinator of a number of the OHI surgical teams, Annette Baldwin shares one of her experiences from a trip to Vanuatu in 2000:

Nursing Influence

I will never forget eight-year-old Samuel, who lived with a serious congenital heart abnormality from birth. He had clubbed fingers, often a symptom associated with the heart condition. Samuel was unable to walk, so his mother carried him on her back everywhere. Even while climbing a rope ladder to scale a volcanic cliff formation in order to reach the garden where Samuel's mother grew the family food, she carried him on her back. A Canadian doctor recognised Samuel's heart condition and advised his mother that when the San's OHI team next visited Vanuatu, she should take Samuel to the capital, Port Vila, to seek help.

This faithful mother listened to the radio every day, hoping she would hear the OHI team was visiting Vanuatu. After two years, she heard the news that the OHI group were in the country. The mother and son lived in the most easterly island in Vanuatu in the province of Tafea, but as soon as she heard the news, she travelled for a week by canoe and boat to the capital to seek help from the OHI team. Samuel was frightened of all the white faces; he had only ever seen a few previously. Samuel and his mum arrived at the beginning of the last week of OHI's visit to Vanuatu and their operating schedule was already full. On learning this mother's story and the effort she had gone to travelling all that way to seek help after waiting so long, the OHI team decided to squeeze the operation into an already full schedule.

The day they operated on Samuel, the first operation commenced at 6 am and the last surgery case finished at midnight. Samuel's congenital heart disease was complex and a challenging surgery to undertake in Port Vila, but OHI teams have extremely skilled and experienced surgeons, anaesthetists, nurses and support staff, who make it possible to undertake such complex operations in remote areas. Samuel made a great recovery and is grateful to the San's wonderfully skilled team of nurses and doctors.

There are many more examples of the impact of OHI teams in many places around the world:

> Dr Charles Sharpe and his wife Margaret pioneered cleft lip and palate surgery in Nepal for OHI. They took San teams to Nepal beginning in the early 1990s and only wrapped up the project in 2004 when insurgents exploded bombs, creating safety concerns for the team. During those years, 109 San nurses travelled to Nepal as part of the OHI teams, which operated on 610 patients who might otherwise have not received reparatory surgery for cleft lip and palates. All OHI team members volunteer their services, use their annual leave and pay their own airfares. Dr Sharpe wrote of his San team surgical visits to Nepal, "We believe that, concerning 'value for money', it was probably one of Australia's best foreign aid programs." Although not an official aid program, it is certainly one example of doctors and nurses having a lasting impact on many lives in other countries as they live out the San's mission for others.

> As well as cardiac services and cleft lip/palate surgery, OHI teams from the San provide plastic surgery for burns victims. In Nepal alone, 625 patients have been treated. Burns are the second most common injury in rural Nepal, accounting for 5 per cent of disabilities. Victims with severe burns develop contractures after inadequate post-burn care. Permanent impairment is common, resulting in restriction of daily living activities. With limited social security in Nepal, no work equals no food. Disfigurement also becomes a social barrier impacting on quality of life for victims.

> In April, 2015, an earthquake struck the Gorkha district in Nepal with an intensity of 7.8 on the Richter scale.

Nursing Influence

Approximately 9000 people were killed and 22,000 injured. Hundreds of thousands of Nepalese were homeless as a result of the destruction. Entire villages were lost. Aulani[5] was a shy 10-year-old girl whose village was destroyed in the earthquake. When the earthquake struck, she was playing between her home and a neighbour's house, but she could not be found after the quake. Eventually Aulani was discovered under a heap of rubble that had fallen on her from collapsing homes. She was badly injured and brought to Scheer Memorial Hospital for care and treatment. One of her wounds healed but with major scarring. During the OHI team's visit to Nepal, Aulani was screened and placed on the list of patients to receive surgical treatment.

Although not a burns victim, the extent of her scarring and contracture prevented her from full use of her hands. Aulani recovered well following her surgery, which released the contractures in her hand and fingers, enabling her to have better functionality and gain more independence.

It is not only the treated individuals who benefit from the San's OHI services, it also benefits their extended families. As the quality of life improves for each of these patients, it also eases the burden on their families.

Over the years, OHI has grown from predominantly providing cardiac surgery to include eye surgery, women's health, burns surgery, orthopaedic surgery, cleft palate surgery and primary healthcare. In a typical year, various OHI teams might visit places such as Mongolia, Vietnam, Fiji, Myanmar, Tanzania, Cambodia and Nepal. Through its nurses, doctors and support staff, the San's influence has spread to many areas of the globe, further illustrating the San's commitment to live out its mission.

For example, in one year alone from July, 2016, to the end of June, 2017, Open Heart International organised 12 medical project visits to six countries and operated on 417 patients who were served by

"Take Me to the San"

272 volunteers from Australia. That year, they paid their first visit to the city of Cochabamba—the fourth largest city in Bolivia—and operated on nine patients. For this project, they worked in partnership with Hospital Univalle and were supported by the Norwest Sunrise Rotary Club of Sydney. The goal of the project and future visits is to foster skill development in cardiology and cardiac surgery for doctors in the Cochabamba region, improve the quality of life for underserved patients unable to access surgery, and to create an exchange program for Bolivian doctors to travel to Australia to gain experience.

The work OHI does in developing countries is a practical expression of the San's mission. While OHI is a San initiative, it has captured the imagination and enthusiasm of nurses, doctors, allied and support staff from much further afield than the San. The OHI program has attracted volunteer team members from Australia, New Zealand and the United States.

From its fledgling beginnings, the San has impacted its local community and abroad in many ways. Training and employing male nurses was a bold step when no other hospital would do so, as was enabling those who wished to gain dual qualifications to train as nurses and ministers of religion. The way San nurses treated and cared for their patients has influenced thousands down through the decades, and many nurses left a lasting legacy by developing San services and facilities in order to better serve the community and the nursing profession. San graduates contributed greatly as medical missionaries, particularly in the South Pacific, and later served in many other parts of the world as part of the San's medical outreach program Open Heart International. These are all innovative programs and different to most hospitals in that the reason behind all this is the San's mission. "Christianity in Action" has long been evident in the way San nurses care for the body, mind and spirit of their patients, as well as those in the broader community and wider world.

Nursing Influence

1. "Men an invisible force in nursing history," *News Issues*, October 16, 2012, <www.apna.asn.au>.

2. H Creighton and F Lopez, "History of Nurse Education in New South Wales," 1982, pages 84–7.

3. Avondale College together with Sydney Adventist Hospital Diploma in Nursing (1976), unpublished, page 21.

4. Ben Wyld, "Insight," *The Sydney Morning Herald*, October 20, 2003, page 11.

5. All patient names have been changed and some personal details omitted to maintain privacy.

San Giving: A Reciprocal Experience

Philip D Currie with Patrina McLean

The San has a long history of reciprocal giving; it both gives and receives in a spirit of philanthropy. Not-for-profit hospitals like the San provide a range of services for the community that the for-profit sector does not typically fund.

Perhaps the longest-standing example of this is the funding the San has provided for training nurses since the hospital opened. More than 100 undergraduate nurses graduate each year, enabling them to become registered nurses. Over the years, many of these nurse graduates have left the San to seek employment in public and private hospitals domestically and internationally. In part, this investment in developing nurses supports the San, but serves the broader community to a greater extent. This investment in nurse training incurs a cost for the San but it is central to its mission.

The San Help Team Volunteers

The San's Help Team is a phenomenal group of 500 volunteers who give their time and skills cheerfully and tirelessly throughout the hospital. These volunteers are mainly retired individuals, but the group also includes former patients, families of patients and people from the local community.

San Giving: A Reciprocal Experience

As a group of volunteers, the Help Team is made up of an array of individuals with differing abilities and personalities, who come together for a common cause—to make a difference in the lives of others and support a hospital they care about. The volunteer program has a strong roster system to support such a large hospital, and each volunteer does a minimum of one four-hour volunteer shift per week. One of the longest-serving members of the Help Team has volunteered at the San for more than 35 years.

Volunteers do many things at the San, such as helping at the front reception desk to guide people around the hospital, restocking supplies in patients' rooms, and supporting patients by delivering newspapers or flowers. Some volunteers drive patients to and from appointments at the San, and others serve snacks and hot drinks to patients receiving treatment in areas like the Day Infusion Centre. Others volunteer in SanSnax, a café from which the profits go toward purchasing life-saving hospital equipment such as humidicribs, oximetry units and other essential pieces needed in theatres, intensive care, the emergency department or general wards. Over the past 10 years, SanSnax has donated $1 million toward such equipment.

A hospital is an environment full of opportunities for kindness. Through volunteering, some find caring a two-way street; care and compassion for others draws focus from their own difficulties and they gain enormous satisfaction themselves. Some volunteers say they've learned the value of "self-care" by volunteering. The companionship and support of the Help Team community and doing good for others gives them a sense of validity and self-worth. Many find that bringing relief and joy to others imparts a sense of happiness and fulfilment.

San volunteers are inspiring and there are many amazing stories of their contribution, including the fact there are ten 90-year-old committed members of the volunteer team, helping out in a variety of roles. They are a much-loved part of the Help Team and the San community.

The contribution many thousands of San volunteers have made

throughout the past century could never be measured. The way the Help Team Volunteers give of their time, skills and resources exemplifies the San's mission.

Health for the community

The San provides many services and facilities for patients and their families that return little or no rebates from government health departments or health funds, but they are services the San considers a crucial part of its mission and service to the community.

In 1993, driven by the vision and passion of Pam Ludowici, the San built an onsite facility called Jacaranda Lodge to offer low-cost, short-term accommodation for patients and their families. This 28-room "home away from home" was built to ease the burden of patients and families who wish to stay close to loved ones in hospital, or those who travel long distances or come from overseas. There are twin, triple and self-contained units, as well as shared kitchen, dining, family rooms and laundry facilities, located 100 metres from the hospital and the Healing Garden.

Jacaranda Lodge also houses the Cancer Support Centre, established in 1993 as a unique community outreach service offering a "one-stop centre" of support services for those undergoing cancer treatment. There are many cancer-specific support groups—such as prostate cancer, breast cancer—education seminars and lectures, counselling, exercise classes, spiritual care services, a drop-in centre, bereavement support and phone support, a wig library and a resource library. Regardless of whether a person is undergoing cancer treatment at the San or another facility, patients and family have access to services within the Cancer Support Centre, most of which are free of charge. This is made possible through a collaboration between the San and the New South Wales Health NGO Grant Program. The San Cancer Support Centre is for anyone, with any cancer type, at any stage of the cancer journey.

The San also regularly holds free health-education forums for the general public including men's health, women's health, nutrition seminars and disease-specific seminars. Throughout the year, it

San Giving: A Reciprocal Experience

also offers free medical update sessions and conferences for general practitioners and allied health providers. This is all part of the San's mission to promote best practice in healthcare and optimum health outcomes for the community.

With the community

Every year, San staff and management join various fundraising initiatives in the local community. These often involve fun, fitness and social interaction to support charitable organisations and humanitarian programs. These include Pink Ribbon Day, Movember, Shave for a Cure, Red Nose Day, Dragons Abreast, Jeans for Genes, Relay for Life, Australia's Biggest Morning Tea, Bobbin Head Cycle Classic, Rotary events and many others. San staff also join with various local churches to provide food and volunteer staff for a food van that distributes food and other necessities for homeless people in the local district.

The San also runs key events of its own. The largest of these is the San Carols, where thousands of people gather on the hospital's front lawn for the annual Christmas carols program. Each year, the San Teddy Bears' Picnic is also held on the front lawn to celebrate mums and dads and the babies born throughout the year. During morning tea and children's entertainment, nurses, midwives, obstetricians and paediatricians get a chance to again see the babies they've delivered and catch up with the parents. In August each year, the San Run for Life attracts families, ex-patients, students from local schools, the community and politicians in a fun run to raise funds for the Cancer Support Centre.

The San gives much to its community and its approach is highly valued. It continues to give even in difficult commercial times, testament to the integrity of the organisation and its mission.

Giving back to the San

The San gives much, but it is also privileged to receive much from grateful patients and community members. This support is greatly appreciated and needed, and helps the organisation achieve greater excellence than it could otherwise achieve. The following are just a few of the many examples that highlight how philanthropists—mostly patients or their families—have given back to the San over the years.

The San has always been a nurse-training institution with student and registered nurses needing accommodation on site. Nurses initially lived in older wooden residences surrounding the hospital. During the 1950s and 1960s, plans were put in place to build a new modern, multi-storey brick nurses' residence behind the hospital. A former San chaplain, Pastor Arthur Knight was commissioned to fundraise for the building program. The nurses' residence was built, with approximately 230 rooms. It has housed thousands of nurses and staff over the years. This facility is remembered by many and its amenity has made a tangible contribution to the life of many nurses and staff, and the hospital as a whole. Pastor Knight fundraised a large portion of the cost to build the new nurses' residence and, thanks to countless donors, the San still uses this facility. In today's building costs, that fundraising effort would equate to many millions of dollars.

The San Foundation was established in 1987 to fundraise and support the work of the hospital in a number of crucial areas. The Foundation raises funds to purchase state-of-the-art equipment to enhance the healthcare provided to patients. It supports San Education through staff scholarships and education grants. It raises funds to support ongoing research projects such as those conducted onsite by the Australasian Research Institute into the causes, prevention and cure of disease. The San Foundation also raises funds for support services for patients and their families.

The San Foundation has provided its community with opportunities to give back. It is well known that many people get to a stage in life where they wish to contribute to benevolent causes. They typically will find a cause that has meaning for them. The San Foundation's role is to provide people with opportunities that give them meaning and fulfil their philanthropic spirit. Giving back to one's community

San Giving: A Reciprocal Experience

is a meaningful expression of gratitude. Linking the desire to give with a personally motivating and emotively engaging project can bring great satisfaction to both the donor and the receiving community.

In 2011, the San embarked on a major expansion and development project. Part of the expansion was the construction of a major new Integrated Cancer Centre onsite. This centre was to physically house many of the key hospital day-only and outpatient cancer-care services. Having all these services in one building would minimise travel distance and inconvenience for patients, as well as enhance professional collaboration for optimal patient care.

The San Foundation took on the challenge and established a target to raise $20 million toward building the Integrated Cancer Centre. Over a period of five years, this target was finally reached and the San Integrated Cancer Centre officially opened in 2017.

The spirit of giving

The San is blessed by a community that is generous in spirit and resources. Donors and philanthropists are inspired by the San, its mission, staff and services. The San is an institution that strives for excellence, with exceptional people achieving exceptional outcomes, many of which are made possible through the generous support of donors. The San is blessed to be a hospital that gives and ultimately receives.

It is fitting we conclude this chapter on giving, with a story about one of the many San philanthropists, as shared by Philip Currie:

> This day was one I had looked forward to with great anticipation for a long time. Driving to work on October 17, 2014, my mind was filled with a sense of satisfaction; today we were celebrating the opening of the new, multi-storey development—the Clark Tower—at the San. The then-Australian Prime Minister Tony Abbott was to officially open the new building. A large white marquee was located in the centre of the front lawn of the hospital, and hundreds of guests were expected. It had been a long

"Take Me to the San"

journey to this point. In 2006, the hospital board had approved the planning of a new series of developments at the San, and today's opening celebrations represented those years of hard work by thousands of people. It was a momentous occasion.

With this air of excitement, I parked in the new multi-level carpark and walked through the entry building. Passing the elevators, the doors opened and, to my delight, Norma Rosenhain and Trevor Roy emerged from the lift. After our friendly acknowledgments, Norma inquired, "How do I get to the Healing Garden?" This was a garden Norma and her family had personally funded and provided high-level supervision for its design and construction beside the San's Integrated Cancer Centre. Knowing the route from the elevators to the garden was somewhat circuitous, I offered to take them there.

Walking from the Integrated Cancer Centre out into the garden, we stopped to admire the garden's features. The Healing Garden has established trees, ground plantings, flowering shrubs, fragrant herbs, seating and tables, grass and private spaces. In the centre of one private space is a large, beautifully polished stone sculpture. Into this stone is etched the facial outlines of Norma's mother and sister—Mrs Dulcie Hunt and Miss Mavis Hunt. Dulcie was a patient at the San shortly before she passed away at home several years earlier. Also etched into the stone is the following text, "The Lord is my Shepherd, I shall not want. He maketh me to lie down in green pastures: He leadeth me beside the still waters. He restoreth my soul..." (Psalms 23:1–3). Norma explained that the inscription was her mother's favourite Bible text. The stylised writing on the stone was in Dulcie's handwriting, taken directly from the Bible Dulcie had written out by hand.

Norma then spoke of her sister, Mavis, who in her early

San Giving: A Reciprocal Experience

20s had passed away at the San with cancer, more than 50 years earlier. This large black polished marble-esque stone, beautifully crafted, sitting proudly in the centre of the Healing Garden, is a personalised and loving memorial to these two precious people, whom Norma dearly loved and remembered.

We walked toward the centre of the garden and stopped. Around the periphery of the garden are a number of large, steel curved panels. Words and graphics are cut out of each solid steel panel. Inspirational texts, phrases and images selected by family members are inscribed on these plates surrounding the garden, creating enclosed, safe places for people who visit the garden to reflect, remember loved ones and seek healing of their spirit. Intimately curated by Norma, the Healing Garden's design and construction is not only a place of personal family healing; it was also intended to be a place for all patients, family, visitors and staff to appreciate. The whole garden is a reflection of what the hospital stands for as a place of healing.

While we stood in the garden looking back toward the entry into the Integrated Cancer Centre, we noted another of these steel panels. On it is the word "Peace" and a cut-out image of a dove. Norma pointed toward the steel plate and said, "That is my panel. Do you know the symbolism of the dove?" she asked.

The question was intended to be rhetorical but, not picking up the nuance, I responded with, "It is used to represent peace and sometimes represents God."

"I'll share with you the meaning of why I placed a dove on my steel panel," Norma continued. "When my sister was in this hospital, she was dying of cancer. We lived close by and our family would come and go from the hospital visiting, spending precious time with Mavis. We loved her dearly and, with palliative care the only treatment left, it

"Take Me to the San"

was only time before she would pass away. One day after vising her, we left for home. While sitting in our lounge room, quite unexpectedly a dove flew through the house and sat on my mother's hand. We did not have any doves, there were no windows or doors open, and we had no idea how the bird got into the house. My mum suggested this was a sign we should go back to the hospital. We left for the hospital and, after being in my sister's room about 30 minutes, she passed away. That is why there is a dove on my panel."

I was moved by Norma's poignant story. And now this dove—a symbol of God's presence—is in the Healing Garden at the San. Not merely a symbol but one born out of a lived experience in connection with a patient in the San and her family members. This was incredibly personal and meaningful to Norma and her family.

With this story, this Healing Garden had become even more meaningful to the San. Norma also reflected that the Healing Garden has been one of her many projects that has brought her the most satisfaction.

The San is a place where people give selflessly of themselves daily. Thousands of complex, simple, unpleasant and pleasant tasks are undertaken daily. The San is a place of giving, inspired by its mission—"Christianity in Action". For every act of giving, there is someone who receives. Some of those who receive the San's spirit of caring and giving reach a point in life when they are happy and able to give back. Some choose to give back to the San through their time, financial support for projects, or leave a legacy such as the story about the dove's significance in the Healing Garden.

Chaplaincy and Spiritual Care

Dr Branimir Schubert, Stenoy (Steve) Stephenson and Dr Alex S Currie

Hospitals are best known for the care of the body and mind; looking after a person's physical and mental health, and treating the pain, injury and disease that confront us as human beings. But the San's mission acknowledges that spiritual care is another crucial dimension of wholistic health and wellness.

Spiritual care is the supportive, compassionate care of people's spiritual and emotional needs during significant times of transition, illness, grief or loss. It is an integral component of wholistic care, requiring a collaborative and respectful partnership between the person and their healthcare provider.[1]

Whether religious or not, all people have "spiritual needs" related to the big questions of life, particularly in the context of ill health, including "Why is this happening to me and what does it all mean? What gives me comfort and hope at this time in my life? Who loves me and is loved by me, no matter what? Who or what is important in my life? What gives my life meaning and purpose?"[2]

There are many facets of spiritual care. Sometimes it involves sitting and listening to patients, family or staff members, or having a conversation or praying with them. Spiritual care can also mean providing access to sacred texts and resources, conducting religious services or rituals, or arranging for religious leaders from that person's faith to visit them in hospital. Spiritual care isn't about imposing one's beliefs on another person, and it makes no assumptions about personal conviction or lifestyle. Spiritual care helps people find meaning, comfort, hope, and a sense of belonging and community during difficult periods in their life.[3]

Spiritual Care Services

The Spiritual Care Services team at the San is a diverse and complementary group that includes professional chaplains, volunteers, spiritual ambassadors (San staff who are spiritual mentors for their peers) and trainees—those doing the supervised chaplains' training component of the Clinical Pastoral Education program. The Spiritual Care team includes visiting representatives from various faiths and denominations who visit their parishioners or community members in hospital. Irrespective of the varying titles, the team provides spiritual care in what was traditionally known as the role of "chaplain" and will generally be referred to as chaplain in the following, for ease of reference.

Chaplains add a significant dimension to the hospital and contribute greatly to its mission. In the following pages, we will look through their eyes at some of the experiences that make up their day-to-day mission of providing spiritual care at the San.

> One weekend I was on-call and a nurse from the oncology ward asked me to visit one of her patients. When I walked into the patient's room, he seemed to be in a contemplative mood. I introduced myself and asked if I could be of help in any way. He explained he'd been sitting there "thinking about life" and wasn't in a good frame of mind, but that maybe it would be good to "just talk."

> He battled tears as he spoke about a difficult few years during which both his parents had died and his marriage dissolved. One day after gardening, he experienced unbearable pain in one of his joints and the pain wouldn't go away. He was admitted to hospital for tests and found to have cancer in a number of places

Chaplaincy and Spiritual Care

throughout his body. Surgery had followed, and now he was facing radiotherapy and chemotherapy.

The patient revealed that he was struggling with the stark reality of his condition, and that "with cancer, some people never make it back home." And then he shared that both his parents had died of cancer on the same ward. While some of the memories were painful, he said being on the same ward brought him a strange kind of comfort.

His tears eased and his face softened as he spoke of one special memory of when he came to visit his parents, both in hospital at the same time. The nurses wheeled his dad into his mum's room, so they could have supper together. He recalled how they both took off their oxygen masks so they could sit side-by-side, talk, and share a cuppa. "It was like a date," he said through fresh tears. "They talked late into the evening, although they were both exhausted." Within the next 24 hours, they both passed away.

What a privilege to spend time listening to this courageous man reflect on the love he had for his parents and the love they had for each other. This deep bond is echoed in the following story.

One night when I was the chaplain on-call at the San, my phone rang while I was fast asleep. I was asked to visit a man in Emergency Care who was dying. When I opened the curtain to the patient's cubicle, I noticed a "Seeing Eye" dog lying at the foot of an elderly gentleman's bed. Sitting in a chair beside the bed was a much younger man dressed in work boots and shorts.

As we talked, the young man said the patient was his father and they were from a property in northern New South Wales. His father fell ill, so he transported him to the closest country hospital more than 100 kilometres from their home. When they arrived at that hospital, they were told there would not be a doctor in attendance for five days, so were advised to drive on. The next

"Take Me to the San"

hospital was unable to admit them due to overcrowding. When the son broke this news to his father—only just conscious by this stage—the father said, "Take me to the San, near Hornsby in Sydney. They looked after me after the war; they will care for me now. I know they will."

After driving many hours, they arrived at the San around midnight. The father was dehydrated, barely conscious and not expected to make it through the night. After talking to the son for a long time, I prayed for his father and told him to call me if his dad deteriorated.

Next morning, this man was still alive. Eventually he stabilised enough to be transferred out of Emergency Care to a ward. Each day the patient grew stronger. After three weeks of care, he recovered and walked out of hospital, led by his faithful guide dog.

A history of spiritual care

Spiritual care at the San is modelled on Jesus' example of ministering to the "whole person"—body, mind and spirit—and has been an integral part of the San's mission since the hospital opened in 1903. American evangelist George Starr served as the hospital's first chaplain from 1903–6. When the hospital opened, there was only one chaplain and approximately 40 staff and 40 patients.

In those days, the official role of chaplains was traditionally carried out by men. However, from the earliest days, women also provided spiritual care at the San, notably Mrs Starr, the wife of the San's first chaplain in 1903. In those days, the women were called Bible workers and did much of a chaplain's work without carrying the title. Now both men and women work as accredited chaplains at the San.

Today the San has 524 licenced beds and cares for more than 186,000 patients each year. More than 4000 people work at the hospital, including 2400 staff, 1100 doctors and 500 volunteers. There are three full-time chaplains, three part-time chaplains,

Chaplaincy and Spiritual Care

six casual chaplains, 34 volunteer chaplains, and 110 Visiting Faith Representatives. In February, 2019, the San received full accreditation as a Clinical Pastoral Education Centre from the New South Wales College for Clinical Pastoral Education. Being a CPE Centre means the San is now formally recognised as being accredited and equipped to offer the professional training course for chaplains and spiritual carers.

The San's Spiritual Care team worked for a couple of years to prepare for the accreditation process. The Accreditation, Registration and Professional Standards Committee of the New South Wales College of Clinical Pastoral Education visited the San to evaluate and assess the San's CPE program eligibility, with the committee unanimously approving the application and the San now registered as a Centre for Clinical Pastoral Education for a period of five years.

The San trains chaplains from all walks of life, including those who work in hospitals, schools and prisons. In 2019, the San also introduced an intensive CPE unit for students who are based interstate or overseas. In response to growing demand, we are working toward running multiple CPE units every year.

This will open many opportunities to train and equip those who look after the spiritual care of people with unique needs, including the sick, their families and staff. It will also open opportunities to provide services we have not been able to provide previously, including more engagement with the local community, and training chaplains and spiritual carers who will serve Australia-wide.

Changing spiritual care

When the San first opened in 1903, it was more of a health and wellness retreat, and patients tended to stay for weeks at a time. Now the hospital is an acute-care institution and the average length of stay in hospital is 5.5 days. While some patients stay for a week or more for complex procedures, some are admitted for as little as a few hours for day surgery. In the context of shorter hospital stays and a more acute healthcare setting, spiritual care plays just as important a role, albeit in a more compressed time frame. The time a patient is in the hospital does not diminish the hospital's focus on its mission—and spiritual care has evolved in response to this changing context.

In 2018, spiritual care services visited 21,824 patients and responded to an additional 549 prayer requests received in prayer books and prayer boxes throughout the hospital. Chaplains care for the spiritual needs of patients and their families, as well as being available to support staff, doctors, volunteers, visitors, contractors and other community members who interact with the San.

Chaplains respect the beliefs and values of each person under their care at the hospital. We are inclusive of all faiths and those of no faith. Spiritual care primarily looks after the "mind" and "spirit" aspects of mission, but these are inseparable from the "body". As we talk with people every day, they open up about their deepest wishes and strongest desires. Recurrent themes emerge: meaning, purpose and value; connection and relationship—with others and with God; and healing and comfort, peace and hope.

These themes are illustrated time and again through patients' poignant stories. As chaplains walk alongside patients and families through some of their most difficult experiences, it is a privilege to see God at work bringing comfort and healing to body, mind and spirit.

Stories of caring

In times of trauma, distress and pain, the questions of meaning and purpose become important in ways they might never have before. Even in a predominantly secular Australian culture, spirituality is significant for 70 per cent of people who are hospitalised. In sharing the stories in this chapter, we relate some examples where people have found it possible to transcend the difficult situations that confront them.

The prayer requests chaplains receive show that many people are seeking comfort, meaning and healing. These prayers are the building blocks of spirituality. Some people want to know what God's will is for their lives. Some have needs in addition to their immediate health issues. Some ask for help with relationship conflict or financial stress, or seek the courage and strength to deal with

Chaplaincy and Spiritual Care

what's ahead of them. In these prayer requests can be heard a longing to make sense of life amid pain, hurt, loss and uncertainty.

Chaplains also receive many thousands of requests each year from patients who wish to be visited on the wards, as illustrated in the following stories.[4]

> There was nothing unusual that evening as I made my rounds of the ward before I signed off for the day. I had one more patient to visit. As I walked into the room, there were at least 15 people around the patient's bed. I was hesitant to interrupt and I thought that, with all those people in the room, my visit would be short. But I was soon engaged in a lengthy conversation with almost everyone present.
>
> When I turned my attention to the patient, everyone else became quiet and the mood in the room suddenly changed. The patient talked about the shock of everything he was going through as a result of his recent diagnosis of terminal cancer. He only had a few weeks to live.
>
> I left the room after more than an hour, promising the patient that I would visit him again. On my third visit, the patient's wife said, "We really like your visits because there is some kind of positive energy you bring into the room."
>
> I visited him regularly. One day when I visited, he was alone. He invited me to sit down. Soon his eyes welled up. He wanted to speak but words didn't seem to come. He was trying his best to hold back the tears but he just couldn't. He talked about a difficult childhood and the decision to work hard so his kids would have a better life. Now, after nearly four decades of hard work, he was on the verge of early retirement with plans to travel the world with his wife. Tickets were booked for their first overseas trip together.
>
> He told me that a few weeks before their much-anticipated holiday, he came to the San for a medical examination

"Take Me to the San"

because of recurring pain. The diagnosis of advanced cancer was beyond shocking to him.

The struggle to cope with this new reality was evident in the patient and his family. Death was knocking at the door of a family who—only days earlier—thought life was fine. That's a hard place to be in.

Part of my job as a chaplain is to talk about whatever the patient wants to talk about, including death, and prepare the patient and family for the inevitable. For the next few days, every evening after his family left, I visited him and we talked about the things on his mind. One evening as we were going through a list of things he needed, all of a sudden he asked me, "What does your faith say about death?" I shared with him about my faith. Two days later, he surprised me when he said, "I'm beginning to pray and talk to your God too. I find a certain peace when I do that. I know I'm dying but I feel closer to God than ever before."

He expressed a need "to do something tangible" as a demonstration of his faith. He was longing for closeness with God. I shared the concept of anointing with him.[5] In my faith community, an anointing ceremony is usually performed when a person is very unwell. Pastors or elders pray with the person before placing oil on the person's head, asking God for healing, courage and comfort. For this patient—a man on his deathbed longing to express his faith in a living God—the concept of anointing brought him comfort.

He talked with his family and, with their consent, we arranged a date for the anointing service in the patient's room. There were prayers and songs, and some of his favourite verses of scripture were read out. As this gentleman's head was anointed with oil, everyone in the room was in tears.

Chaplaincy and Spiritual Care

A few days later, I received a phone call with the news I had expected but dreaded—he had passed away. I helped the family make arrangements for the funeral and supported them as best I could. As I was standing at the nursing station, I turned to see the patient's wife and family on their way out of the hospital. Before I spoke a word, she said, "I am leaving this hospital with the hope of meeting my husband again because of what was done for him the other day." She was referring to the anointing service. She left the San with hope beyond this world.

Anointing is just one way to meet the spiritual and emotional needs of a patient. Chaplains strive to find what is most relevant and meaningful to the needs of each person. It is an enormous privilege and responsibility to be entrusted with the spiritual care of people; to listen, to be present, to create a safe space for people to share and reflect.

It was a cold and rainy evening when I came to work, and the intensive care unit was busy. When I walked into the patient's room to introduce myself, he was alert and watching the activity around him. I told him my name and my role as a chaplain and asked if he would like me to stay and visit with him for a while.

"Of course, please sit down." He then asked me a strange question. "I thought you came just to visit me, but if you are a hospital chaplain, you will be visiting other patients too, right?"

I explained that I do see other patients during my rounds, but that my time was all his.

"Today is an unforgettable day for me," he said. "When you walked in, I thought you were especially coming to visit me. You see, I had a dream last night that someone came to visit me and we spent time talking. It was a strange dream. Anyway, I am glad to have a visitor."

"Take Me to the San"

I asked him why today was an unforgettable day and he said it was the second anniversary of his daughter's death, as well as being the 25th anniversary of his wife's death.

"The anniversaries being the same date makes it unbearable; I don't know who to mourn." At this point, he became teary. It seemed he was on his own. His remaining family—another daughter—lived interstate and was also unwell.

"Yesterday, I was wishing someone would visit me, and today my wish is fulfilled. My life is nearing its end; I'm ready to go. But do you believe in prayer? Can you pray for me and my remaining daughter? I never believed in God, especially after my wife died. But would you say a prayer."

And so I prayed: "Our Father and our God, the One who is in control of life. We come before You now with our hearts weighed down as a result of the storms of life. But yet we call on You because You are the light, and You can shine brightly into our lives so we may find meaning, find hope and find purpose. The very fact Your child—this man—has asked for prayer speaks volumes of his renewed trust and belief in a living God. A God who is in control of the future, a God of love, a God who cares, a God who is interested in each of our personal lives. May the belief in You, God, be a river of living water flowing up to eternal life. May all the pain, wounds, brokenness and emptiness be filled with Your comfort, and may the Spirit of peace, love, healing, grace, mercy and health fill the hearts and home of this man and his daughter. I ask all these things in the matchless name of Jesus Christ. Amen."

When I had finished praying, the patient asked me, "Can I have a hug?"

"Sure," I replied—and we hugged. Then he took my hand and looked me in the eyes and said, "Last night I had a dream. I didn't know that it was you who I saw in my dream, I just saw a man visit me. He told me he had a message from God. He told me the message and left me after hugging me. The reason I asked you to pray just now was to make sure that it was you that God sent in my dream. And you used the same words in your prayer just now, that the man said to me last night in my dream. This morning when I woke up, I was shaken. I asked the nurse for a pen and paper and wrote down what that man told me was a message from God to me."

He then reached over, pulled a piece of paper from under his pillow, and gave it to me. "Here, read it—that's what God told me."

There was a long moment of silence as I read what he'd written on the piece of paper. As I finished reading and looked back at his face, he smiled and said, "Thank you for coming. God sent you here. You made my day."

When people are in hospital, they're often confronted with their fallibility and loss of control. They are cut off from familiar surroundings and from those they love. They're forced by circumstance to take stock of the fact some relationships aren't what they hoped they might be. There can be a real sense of urgency to heal rifts in relationships, sort out grievances and put family affairs in order.

Particularly when faced with grave illness or death, there can be a heightened sense of wanting to experience love, forgiveness and connection. Spirituality encompasses all these key aspects of human need. Chaplains come alongside patients with compassion, in prayer, with conversation.

Sometimes random conversations with patients spark friendships and create connections between groups of people who would otherwise never meet. One such conversation between a patient and a chaplain led to a new friendship in Sydney that had flow-on effects in remote communities of the Solomon Islands. In this case,

"Take Me to the San"

part of the San's mission—caring for community—reached some 3000 kilometres across the ocean.

The patient was a businessman, he informed me when I walked into his room. We chatted for a while and I told him it was my first day back at work after visiting the Solomon Islands for two weeks. He asked why I went to the Solomon Islands, and I shared with him that each year I help organise a team of tradespeople and high school students to travel to the Solomons to improve infrastructure in schools.

"Why?" he asked.

"Because I see education as a basic and necessary foundation for young people to obtain a career and work."

"So what kind of infrastructure do you put into these schools?" the patient asked.

"We work on remote high schools; you could call them bush schools. If they need electricity generators, we install them. If they need water supplies, we pump water from rivers and reticulate it through the school compound. If guttering and water tanks are needed, we install them. In fact, the school we worked on during this trip had three water tanks for 250 students and staff. Our plumber, working with the local people, installed eight tanks and guttering to capture rainwater. The team built two ablution blocks with 10 flush toilets each, showers, clothes-washing sinks, and room to hang clothes indoors when it rains."

The patient asked me, "What kind of taps did you use?"

"I have no idea, but I can tell you what they look like—I have a photo of them on my iPad," I replied.

I showed him a picture of the taps and he exclaimed, "These are the taps that I produce. Next time you go to the

Solomon Islands on one of these projects, I will supply all the taps and much more." And he did.

It is incredible where conversations can lead. When asked to visit an elderly woman on the ward, one chaplain had a brief conversation with her granddaughter as he was leaving the patient's room. This sparked a profound exchange between granddaughter and grandmother that deepened the relationship between them.

> One day after talking and praying with a lovely 93-year-old woman, I walked out of the room and saw a young woman leaning against the wall, texting on her phone. When she saw me, she asked, "Is my grandmother dying?"
>
> Thinking for a few seconds, I replied, "I am not a medical doctor and cannot really answer your question, but your grandmother is preparing to die."
>
> She asked, "Chaplain, what can I do to help my grandma feel at peace?"
>
> I suggested she write a letter to her grandmother, thanking her for all the good times they'd enjoyed together and for everything she had taught her. "And perhaps you could let your grandma know that the memories she made will stay with you for the rest of your life," I added.
>
> The next day when I visited, the patient shared with me a beautiful letter her granddaughter had written. There were tears in her eyes.
>
> A couple of days later, this grand old lady passed peacefully to rest.

There are times when patients just want someone to listen to them without judgment or questions or interruption. Chaplains know they can't possibly solve every problem, nor are they expected to, but they know how important it is for people to feel heard.

> As I approached the patient, he looked like he was in the middle of his lunch, but he was just sitting in a chair,

"Take Me to the San"

holding a cup in his hand and not moving. He looked downcast. I asked whether he'd like me to spend some time with him. When he raised his head, I could see tears in his eyes as he began to talk. "I'm just waiting to die," he said. "I have no-one; it's only me and God now. I'm waiting for Him and I don't know how much longer."

There was deep pain and hurt in his eyes when he spoke of the death of his wife and estrangement from his adult children. "Ever since then," he said, "I have been alone in this world. At one stage, I began to feel depressed. I became very sick and I was close to death at least three times. But those were the times I began to have a great relationship with God. I experienced something I have never experienced before—God was always with me and I didn't feel as lonely anymore.

"This time in the hospital is unlike before; I know I won't go home this time. My priest came in the other day and prayed with me. See this body, it's too old and tired. I am ready to go. Anyway, I'm getting tired now and I can't sit for long. I didn't give you a chance to speak. I did all the speaking. But thank you for coming in, I wasn't expecting a visitor. I greatly appreciate what you are doing. Son, be faithful to your God. Be of good courage in this world and be happy, for God is with you."

It was a blessing to meet this elderly gentleman. He had experienced a lot of heartache and hurt, yet he seemed to be a man of courage, love and compassion. He had risen above difficult life experiences and was certain about God. He had built a great relationship with God that seemed to sustain him through the toughest times.

Being part of the healing process is a privilege. Skilled, committed doctors and staff work incredibly hard to achieve the best outcomes for their patients through treatments and surgery. Many things can be done to ease physical pain and suffering. But the prospect of facing

Chaplaincy and Spiritual Care

a prolonged illness or death creates immeasurable distress in other ways. In these times, emotional and spiritual comfort is paramount. Spiritual care is about coming alongside someone with compassion. It is a way to help people find a measure of comfort and peace, and to know they are in safe hands.

A place of prayer

The San chapel is an important place of reflection and connection within the hospital. It is a peaceful space that attracts people of all backgrounds, religions, races and creeds. For many, the hospital chapel is the heart and soul of the hospital. Whoever you are, wherever you come from and at whatever point of your spiritual journey you are on, you are welcome in the chapel, "For My house will be called a house of prayer for all the people" (see Isaiah 56:7).

The chapel is used occasionally for baby dedications, family blessings, weddings, funerals and memorial services. On the first Friday of every month, a "Healing and Restoration" service is conducted in the chapel, sharing stories of healing and restoration, followed by fellowship and refreshments. Regular "Sabbath Praise" programs are also held in the chapel, focusing on the healing power of music and song. These programs can be viewed on the TV in patients' rooms to encourage and inspire.

There is always a prayer book in the chapel in which people can write their prayer requests, anonymously or otherwise. Those who work in spiritual care in the hospital setting sometimes see miracles of healing that sustain and strengthen their own faith. This is one such account, when many people witnessed a rapid turnaround in a patient's condition.

> It was late one Friday evening when I received a call alerting me that there was a patient in trouble. A mum and her newborn baby were in crisis. I knew some of my colleagues and friends were in the hospital, so I sent an urgent text message asking for the cover of prayer. Within minutes of receiving this text message, a small group of hastily assembled nursing staff, chaplains, managers

"Take Me to the San"

and support staff huddled in the hospital chapel to pray for this mother and new baby. Prayers extended to the doctors and staff caring for them, and to the family. A few members from a local church, who happened to be in the hospital foyer, also joined the prayer. God's help was desperately sought; His promises were claimed. Gradually, the chapel emptied and people went home. The next morning, there were tears of gratitude and much joy when the message filtered out that the mother and baby's condition was stable.

Those special occasions

There is no such thing as an average day for a chaplain. Each situation is different and chaplains are usually in the thick of human distress and discomfort. But sometimes they are pleasantly surprised when called to use talents they might never have imagined they had—such as being a wedding planner.

A middle-aged woman was admitted to the San and, following extensive medical checks, she received the dreaded news that her condition was terminal and that she would most likely die within two weeks. Her daughter was due to get married in a few months, which added another dimension of distress at the prospect of not being there for the wedding.

The daughter desperately wanted to bring forward the wedding so her mother could share the special day. They asked the chaplains if a wedding could be arranged in the hospital chapel. Negotiations were made, her priest was able to conduct the wedding, and the mother was wheeled into the chapel on her bed—to the applause of gathered family, staff and well-wishers. It was a beautiful, poignant wedding service.

The patient passed away within a few days, but the ward staff and chaplains who moved mountains to make the

Chaplaincy and Spiritual Care

wedding happen in time, helped fulfil the wish of a daughter and her dying mum.

A chaplain describes a wedding he helped organise on another occasion for one of his patients, which demonstrates that love and comfort can indeed triumph, despite facing death.

> The conversation with the patient, John, and his partner, Jane, started out with a great discussion about favourite travel destinations and what we loved about particular holiday destinations in favourite countries. After we'd chatted for about 10 minutes, John's voice became emotional and he said softly, "I'm not going to leave hospital. I have terminal cancer and the prognosis is that I will die within three or four weeks."
>
> I paused, uncertain what would be the best thing to say in this circumstance. So I simply said, "I'm so sorry. How can I best help you?"
>
> John spoke in subdued tones, but was soon overcome with emotion. Jane then explained what he was trying to say. "John and I have lived together for many years. We had always promised each other we would get married, but we've both been too busy working, running a business and travelling, and we haven't fitted marriage into life's equation. But as a dying wish, John is asking if you would marry us in the hospital chapel."
>
> "Of course I will," I replied. "One hitch could be the government—there are strict rules around marriage. Normally a couple is required to wait 30 days after signing papers of intent to marry, before they can marry. However, yours is a special circumstance and I will try to negotiate around those rules for you."
>
> I phoned the New South Wales Registry of Births, Deaths and Marriages, and it was suggested I make an application to Hornsby Court House to marry the couple as soon as

"Take Me to the San"

possible. After three visits to the court house, I finally received the necessary papers on Friday. Not knowing when John might pass away, we planned the wedding for Saturday afternoon.

John arrived at the chapel in a wheelchair, dressed in suit and tie, looking very dapper. I had never seen him dressed like this; previously I'd only seen him in hospital gowns or pyjamas. Jane arrived with her father. She looked stunning. The hospital chapel was beautifully decorated. Friends and family gathered to celebrate with this delightful couple. Everyone rallied to help make the occasion extra special. The atmosphere was emotionally charged, recognising John's life was limited and that this service was a death-bed wish and the result of a long-standing promise the couple made to each other.

After the wedding ceremony, well-wishers filled the beautiful atrium garden attached to the cancer ward, where the couple relaxed with family and friends to share moments of sheer joy and happiness.

John passed away a week later. One of this couple's last wishes—to be married—had been fulfilled, and everyone in attendance was touched by their powerful demonstration of love.

Bringing comfort and support

It is not only the momentous occasions in life where spiritual care makes a difference. Sometimes it only takes one small sentence, asking one question, to bring comfort and peace to a patient.

Dropping into a room one morning while on rounds, I found a young woman sitting in a chair gazing out the window. After I introduced myself as a chaplain, she shared a wonderful story about how a seemingly small gesture from a nurse the night before had brought her comfort.

Chaplaincy and Spiritual Care

> This young patient had been admitted to hospital the previous evening and was experiencing severe pain, despite medication. She was naturally quite distressed and upset. A nurse came into the room, tried to comfort her and then said, "Would you like me to pray to God that He will take away the pain and give you peace of mind and a calm spirit?"
>
> The patient said she replied to the nurse, "I have never had a Christian pray for me. But if you would like to pray for me, I would like that."
>
> This young patient said the experience meant so much to her. She relaxed, the pain left her and she slept well. When I spoke to her, she was in a contemplative and appreciative mood. In this case, as in many others, nurses become the spiritual conduits of God's grace and His healing power.

Working in spiritual care can have its stressful, difficult moments. Despite that, chaplains reflect that it is a privilege and an honour to be a part of the hospital's mission; to be the "hands and feet" of a loving, living God, who is the ultimate healer, comforter, and a lasting source of peace and hope.

> I was on call, it was the middle of the night and I had just spent time with a grieving family who had lost a loved one. As I left that ward and got into the elevator, another patient came into my mind. I had visited him many times previously and he mentioned he was often unable to sleep at night. Although it was 2 am, I was impressed to check in on this patient, in the off-chance he was having one of his sleepless nights.
>
> When I quietly walked into his room, it was clear he was awake. As soon as he saw me, he said, "This is no coincidence that you are here at this time. I am so troubled, so uncomfortable, I can't sleep. I need your help." He started crying. I sat down beside him and

"Take Me to the San"

listened as he poured out his heart. Here lay a relatively young man on his deathbed. Not only was he in physical pain, he was suffering a great deal of mental anguish.

Eight months prior, this man went to his doctor to have a relatively minor procedure. What followed was a cycle of pain; biopsies revealed he had an aggressive cancer. He had multiple surgeries and wounds that would not heal.

He had spent eight months in excruciating pain, bedridden, hopelessly searching for a cure. He was faced with two options: with active treatment, he had an estimated lifespan of one year; without treatment, he could die quite soon.

He had made the choice to stop active treatment, which meant he would likely die sooner, rather than suffer excruciating pain and be bedridden for another year before the inevitable happened. He had wrestled long and hard with these options. We talked many times about his family dynamics, his financial situation, his spirituality, his priorities and values.

I spent time talking with his wife and young son. The son stunned me with the maturity he exhibited. He was bold, brave and courageous when he was in front of his father. He talked and laughed, as they shared jokes. One day the son and I walked down to the café for a break. As we sat down, even before I could ask my first question, the boy burst into tears. It was too difficult for him to accept that his dad wouldn't be coming home ever again. It was hard to accept that his dad has just a few more weeks ahead of him. He had questions: Why? Why now? Why my dad?

When we returned to the patient's bedside, the boy looked in his father's eyes and said, "Dad, I may not have told you this before, but I want you to know that you are my hero. Even though I play video games and talk about super heroes, in my life I have only one hero—and that's you." They embraced and talked, sharing memories and how important they were to each other.

And now here I was on-call, in the hospital lift, and had been impressed to visit this gentleman even though it was 2 am. When I walked into his room, he told me what had been troubling him so much. He shared that a friend of his had visited him earlier that evening and told him that he was committing suicide; that by not accepting active treatment, he was choosing to die. What a devastating thought to have on top of everything else he was going through. He was very troubled.

"God was never a part of my life," the patient said. "I never thought I needed God before. I think there is a God somewhere but I have nothing to do with Him." He had been battling alone with these thoughts for hours. A heart-touching conversation followed. We talked about life, death, suicide, cancer, his current situation, the choices he had made. We talked about God—a God of love and comfort.

A few days later, at his request, we held a special service for him in his room, inviting his family and the ward staff who had been caring for him. Just as we were concluding the service, he asked that we sing the song "What a friend we have in Jesus". This song expressed the friendship he had built with God on his deathbed; a friendship that was a source of comfort, hope and peace for a man who endured the most wretched suffering.

A few days later, he breathed his last breath. I bade farewell to a man who had become infinitely less like a patient and more like a long-lost brother I had the privilege of getting to know in the most trying hours of his life.

There are many occasions when chaplains are asked to support patients and staff through times of grief and when they are

"Take Me to the San"

confronted with the tragedies of life: pain, accidents, injury, death and dying. Peace is something Jesus offered His followers, "Peace I leave with you" (John 14:27), while the apostle Paul described it as a "peace...that passes all understanding" (Philippians 4:7). An important role of spiritual care is helping people find a measure of comfort and peace despite their circumstances.

As one of the chaplains visited an elderly patient on the ward following surgery, the patient shared an experience that had been meaningful to her.

> When I visited the patient, she was a few days after surgery. As we got talking, she said that she had been very worried about the anaesthetic and the surgery before the operation, but had been uplifted by an experience that took place in the operating theatre.
>
> She was met in the ante-room of theatres by the anaesthetist who had come to see her and prepare her for the anaesthetic. As the anaesthetist came through the swinging doors from the theatres, the patient noticed a "waft" of music coming from the adjoining room. She remarked that she could hear nice music, and the anaesthetist explained that the surgeon liked to have music in the background while he operated.
>
> The anaesthetist then asked the patient if she liked music, to which she replied, "Yes, I love music!" He asked her what music or song she liked best of all, and she said, "'New York, New York' by Frank Sinatra".
>
> The anaesthetist stopped what he was doing and politely asked to be excused for a minute. A few moments later he returned and opened both of the swinging doors between the operating theatre and the room where the patient was waiting. He asked if she could hear the music. He had found her favourite song "New York, New York" on Spotify and was playing it for her as she was going under the anaesthetic. She said it settled her

apprehension, and she greatly appreciated this gesture of care and attention.

Whether the person's experience in hospital was a difficult one involving injury, illness or surgery, or a joyous one—such as the birth of a baby—the basic human needs of meaning, purpose and value; connection and relationship; healing, comfort, peace and hope are magnified like they are in perhaps no other setting. The San's mission—"Christianity in Action: Caring for the body, mind and spirit of our patients, colleagues, community and ourselves"—is embodied in every aspect of spiritual care.

1. Spiritual Health Victoria, 2016, page 7, <www.spiritualhealthvictoria.org.au>.

2. University of Maryland Medical Center, <https://www.umm.edu/patients/pastoral/what-is-spiritual-care>.

3. Spiritual Care Australia, <www.spiritualcareaustralia.org.au/SCA/AboutUs>.

4. All patient names have been changed and some personal details omitted to maintain privacy.

5. Biblical Research Institute, "The Anointing Service," <www.adventistbiblicalresearch.org/materials/practical-christian-living/anointing-service>.

Mission Shapes Our Vision for the Future

Brett Goods

As I was writing this chapter, I received an email from a patient that reminded me again of the importance of the San's mission and vision, and the effect they have on those who interact with the organisation:

> It is with deep gratitude and much appreciation that I write to you. I spent a number of weeks in the San at different times recently and I can honestly say that the genuine care, compassion and dedication to patient comfort and wellbeing cannot be adequately complimented in words. This culture was evident from every team member, including cleaners, food providers, trainees, nurses, supervisors, wardsmen, pathologists, doctors and specialists.
>
> You can be extremely proud of what your team provides for patients and their families at traumatic and uncertain times. Each and every one that I came in contact with, or saw come in contact with other patients, displayed and exercised a culture of care and patient wellbeing of an exceptional standard.

Mission Shapes Our Vision for the Future

I won't single out individuals who were involved in my care, as there are always some who go above and beyond—as was the case many times during my stay. Suffice to say, I never experienced a single team member who did not "pull their weight."

At the reception on the second level (Clark Building) and at reception in the Hub, certain values and aims are either carved into the desk or displayed on the wall. Those "pillars" are evident in your amazing hospital team who have "bought into" and executed the hospital's mission and values.

I thank the team involved in my care. While I was experiencing a difficult and stressful time, their contribution made it easier to endure and was—and is—gratefully appreciated.

Reflecting on this email and the impact mission has had on the San's history—as described in the previous chapters of this book—mission continues to hold a central place in shaping the vision for the organisation into the future. With the other members of the executive and leadership team, we stand on broad shoulders and we want to build on the hospital's legacy. As we consider the present and approaching challenges in the healthcare sector, we are always looking for new opportunities to serve our community better. An inspiring vision and a clear strategic plan for how to achieve that vision is crucial to the organisation's success.

The challenges of healthcare

Before we explore the San's vision and the strategies necessary to achieve that vision, it is helpful to have an understanding of the status quo within the broader healthcare landscape across Australia currently.

The acute healthcare sector in Australia is facing a number of significant challenges, including a greater demand for healthcare services due to the ageing population, increasing costs of private health insurance, and an overloaded public hospital system. The

"Take Me to the San"

gap payments or out-of-pocket costs associated with doctors' consultations is causing consumer angst. And Australia has a diminishing pool of "healthy insured": the number of healthy young people with private health insurance is dwindling, as they weigh up the value of having private health insurance when making decisions about disposable income and cost-of-living pressures.

Intersecting these stressors is the exponential burden of chronic disease, much of which is lifestyle related. Private hospitals are also experiencing pressure from private health insurers because the amount insurers pay hospitals for each episode of care does not match the increased costs each year to deliver that care, requiring productivity gains—meaning, cost savings—to balance these impacts.

There is broad acknowledgment things have to change in the way we deliver healthcare in this country. As things stand in Australia, an obese 80-year-old with multiple co-morbidities pays the same private health insurance premiums as an Olympic athlete. Or they could both choose not to have private health insurance at all, and they'd still receive equal access to "free" healthcare through Medicare and the public health system. Apart from a person's own desire to be healthy, there is little reward or incentive to be. Knowing we have access to public healthcare, at "no cost" to us, perhaps decreases motivation for self-responsibility.

Hospitals have to continue to work with governments and private health insurers to explore opportunities to maximise the health impact of limited dollars. In this environment, the need to influence people's management of their health outside of hospitals will require greater emphasis. More energy and focus will be put into disease prevention and health promotion. These measures will be about promoting better health and quality of life, as well as trying to reduce the time people spend in hospitals.

A phenomenon that has grown over the past decade, and more aggressively in the past few years, is what has been called "privatisation of public hospitals by stealth."[1] In public hospitals, there are administrative staff whose role it is to encourage people who have private health insurance to sign into public hospitals as private patients. This means the cost of the patient's stay in the public hospital is met by the private health insurer via the patient's premiums. Which also means the government benefits because the private health insurer covers the cost of the patient's admission to public hospital, not the government. Research shows pressure is applied to patients to use their private health insurance in public hospitals even in metropolitan areas where there are many private hospital options nearby.[2]

The rates of elective surgery in public hospitals for privately insured patients has gone up markedly, far exceeding those of public patients. A report in 2018 showed that private elective admissions to public hospitals increased by 153 per cent, compared with 24 per cent for public patients.[3] And more and more women with private health insurance are choosing to have their babies in public hospitals to save out-of-pocket expenses. A number of private hospitals across Australia have closed or consolidated their maternity units as a result, leaving patients with fewer options and more pressure on public maternity units.

The number of private health insurance-funded hospitalisations in public hospitals increased on average nearly 10 per cent each year over the 10 years to 2016.[4] According to research conducted by the Australian Institute of Health and Welfare, the amount private health insurers pay for private patients being treated in public hospitals is $1.5 billion each year.[5] This places upward pressure on private health insurance premiums.

According to a report in 2018, more than 800,000 episodes of care in public hospitals were funded by private health insurance in one year alone.[6] This is potentially 800,000 episodes of care that could have been done in private hospitals, leaving 800,000 opportunities for public patients—those without private health insurance—to be treated in a more timely manner in those public hospital beds.

Promoting health

A different approach to healthcare is needed if people are to receive affordable quality care and maintain good health into the future. The impact of not just an ageing population but an unhealthy ageing population and the full impact of lifestyle-related chronic diseases will put even greater strain on hospitals. In order to bring long-term change to the way the Australian healthcare system currently operates, a multi-disciplinary effort will be required to increase collaboration, to jointly influence governments and private health insurers, to harness research, to drive new initiatives, and to promote health and wellbeing more broadly in the community.

The current Australian healthcare framework presents challenges—due to legislation and funding—that hinder the broader adoption of health and wellbeing promotion in the acute hospital context. As things stand, Medicare and private health insurers provide few rebates for non-acute or health-promoting initiatives done in the hospital setting. And Australia's health system doesn't offer particularly well resourced out-of-hospital health-promoting activities for people who've had acute health episodes and are now back in the community.

Private hospitals are significantly restricted by Medicare rules and government legislation and private health funds to only provide services they consider to be hospital services. Sadly, this means many health-promoting initiatives are excluded. But there are—and will be—opportunities to partner with insurers and technology providers to trial variations to the current models of care.

The San has been providing health-promoting services as part of its core mission since 1903, including dietitians, physiotherapy, massage, exercise physiology, cardiac rehabilitation, general rehabilitation, social workers, psychologists, spiritual care services and public health education. With cardiac disease, for example, the San provides acute intervention cardiac surgery, as well as cardiac rehabilitation. Combined, this results in better outcomes for the patient. Exercise incorporated into cancer treatment leads to better outcomes, and we continue to see positive links between exercise and better mental health. These are just a few examples.

Most patients are in hospital for less than a day or two; most often, those who stay longer are acutely unwell. For health promotion, this means we have to engage with our patients not only inside the acute hospital setting but outside the hospital as well. We hold health forums for the community: men's health, women's health, mental health, cancer, cardiac, dietetics—to name a few. We hold education sessions for doctors in general practice. We promote a healthy lifestyle and have made evidence-based changes in the foods we serve to both community and staff. And as part of our mission to care for the mind and spirit, our spiritual care service has initiated a program where they aim to visit every patient who spends a night in the hospital.

At the San's Integrated Cancer Centre, patients receive wholistic care in a multi-disciplinary model. They can see their cancer specialist, then walk across the hallway for blood tests, scans and X-rays, chemotherapy, radiotherapy, counselling, and support services—all in the one location. Within the cancer centre, we also have a clinical trials unit and a genetic screening service. An outdoor healing garden was built adjacent to the cancer centre where patients and families can spend time in a tranquil natural environment.

Most of the cancer support is offered as a community service. We cannot get Medicare or private health insurance rebates for the majority of these supportive services. Some of the costs are absorbed by the hospital, supported through grants and donations and, in some cases, patients contribute a small fee—but most services are free. It's part of our mission to provide more wholistic care for our community. And people don't even have to have been treated for cancer at the San in order to take part in the Cancer Support Services; they're available to the general community. Why do this? Because it's proven to produce significantly better patient outcomes and quality of life.

Teamwork

Another San initiative is the expansion of multi-disciplinary teams (MDT). Multi-disciplinary teams are groups of doctors, specialists and allied health professionals who meet together regularly to discuss patients' diagnoses and use evidence-based guidelines to plan the best treatment options. The concept is not new to the hospital—they've been running at the San for decades—but we've recently upped the ante with a purpose-built MDT centre co-located with the new Integrated Cancer Centre.

The team meets in a high-tech room where the patient's condition, pathology results and X-rays can be viewed and discussed as a group with the patient's consent. Rather than a patient having just one doctor's opinion, a broad range of experts and input provides the patient with the optimum treatment plan, in which the patient is actively involved.

Evidence shows that an MDT approach to a person's care can reduce mortality and improve quality of life. Not only are patients getting the best clinical care, they're also more comprehensively supported by allied health, social work, specialist nurse navigators and counselling.

Only a small fee can be claimed for these MDT sessions. All of the MDT participants give their time voluntarily, and most of the cost is absorbed by the hospital. Why do this? Because it is proven to be enormously beneficial for the patient and leads to better outcomes. It also builds knowledge and collegiality between the medical, clinical and support personnel. It is all part of considering the whole person in our care, and driving continued improvement, excellence and high-quality care.

Future mission

We know the increasing health costs are unsustainable. The ageing population is inevitable. Chronic preventable disease is a reality. There is greater pressure to reduce length of hospital stays. Health dollars are stretched to capacity. But, despite that, more focus has to go toward strategies to prevent admissions to hospital and to keep people living more healthfully in society.

How to get people to take greater responsibility for their own health is an age-old problem, but supporting them on that journey is crucial. Research is emerging that technology can be useful to get greater individual buy-in of wellbeing initiatives, particularly with wearable smart devices, apps and in-home monitoring. Any health-promoting activity has to factor in what is culturally appropriate, the social impact and the environment people are living in—and try to do all this while being good stewards of finite resources.

The San is looking to draw more on our long-standing focus on wellbeing and wellness. This will be one of our key differentiators into the future. There is more we could be doing in education, exercise, lifestyle measures and health promotion. Given the short time patients spend in hospital these days, we'll also be looking at what more can be done outside the hospital setting, and how these initiatives will be funded. We will continue to partner with other well known, globally respected organisations for wellbeing innovations. This will help move us from a sick-care system to a true health-care system.

Vision

Stories from our past inspire our mission for today and our vision for the future. These stories are of people who made the San's mission come alive and touched the lives of countless people in our community and beyond. So how do we continue to build on the strong foundations the San has, to respect that legacy while still being agile enough to move boldly ahead amid the challenges and opportunities of the times we're in?

Despite the healthcare, policy and economic challenges, we are pursuing a bold vision for the San, while keeping our mission focus. Our mission is why the San exists, but our vision is where we want the organisation to be into the future. In crafting the vision for the organisation, it needed to be simple, short, understandable, motivating and relatable. So—in March, 2019—our board approved the San's new vision: "To be a thriving, faith-based provider of world-class care, inspiring hope and wellbeing."

For it to be relatable, compelling and motivating, each person has to find some way to connect with the vision. This way, each person will have a touchstone within that vision, personally and when interacting with others. With my wife's blessing, I shared with our staff some of the ways the vision has real meaning for me.

"Take Me to the San"

In December, 2018, my wife was diagnosed with breast cancer, which was a shock to her at the age of 50 and otherwise healthy. As we were considering treatment options, I wanted for my wife a place where we could have confidence she would receive world-class care. I wanted to know she was in a place where staff and doctors had exceptional skills, had faith in God, and where they valued excellence. I wanted her to be in a hospital that was thriving, and where people and services embodied care, dignity and integrity.

An ex-nurse who had worked at the San for 21 years, my wife knew it was a place that cares for the body, mind and spirit; a place that inspires hope and wellbeing. We know this organisation has world-class people and services, so when we were considering treatment options, there was no choice for us except the San. For me personally—as a husband and as CEO of the San—there is real significance in the San's vision statement.

We know the San has had a much-loved and well respected reputation during its long history. We know the organisation does many fantastic things and that we have world-class elements to the services we provide. We also know that we're not perfect. There are always opportunities to do better across an array of things we do, how we do them and how we work as teams to deliver care for our community.

To reiterate, the San's vision is: "To be a thriving, faith-based provider of world-class care, inspiring hope and wellbeing."

- **Thriving**

We want the San to be a thriving organisation, including individuals and departments that grow and flourish. We want organisational health and financial health. We want positive interactions with patients and their families and relationship health internally within our teams: focused on how people treat each other and interact with each other.

Outside the organisation, it's about how we relate to the community and whether we're a good corporate citizen. We want to have the right guidelines, processes and procedures in place to protect our patients, staff, reputation and excellence. And one of our strategic focus areas is for our staff to be engaged, achievement-focused, and personally and professionally fulfilled.

In the San's vision statement, "thriving" is intended in a wholistic way: the San is an organisation that thrives as it organically and sustainably delivers on its promise to care for the body, mind and spirit.

- **Faith-based**

The San was established by people of the Seventh-day Adventist faith—responding to the needs of the Sydney community in 1903—who were committed to providing wholistic care for people. This mission has been a constant throughout the San's history, and we want that to continue as an integral part of our vision into the future.

The San's mission and values are based on faith and belief in God, striving to reflect the way God cared for people in the way we care for people. However, we want to make a lasting difference in people's lives irrespective of their nationality or beliefs, whether they express a particular faith or no faith. Similarly, our staff don't have to be of a particular faith to be engaged, values-aligned and make a difference to people and the organisation.

The Adventist Church has been a constant throughout the San's history and there are many stories in this book about how God has blessed the San at times when things seemed difficult. And I believe that God is blessing the organisation now, even though the healthcare industry is again in one of those difficult times.

We want this link with faith and our history to be ongoing in our vision for the organisation into the future. We are driven by an imperative to bring relief and hope to people. And I believe this is achieved through the cooperation of human effort and divine power. In the San's mission, we often refer to the concept of extending Christ's ministry of health and healing to our patients and community.

"Take Me to the San"

- **World-class**

Our vision of maintaining world-class standards is about being outstanding. We already achieve outstanding results in many areas, but there are always opportunities for us to improve and to be more consistent in the way we deliver care. We want to maintain an international standard of excellence in our services, and we know that in order to do that, we have to attract world-class people to work in the organisation. We want to have a consistency across all aspects of the business: mission, values, people, vision and strategy.

- **Care**

Yes, we're a hospital, and healthcare is an obvious element of what a hospital does, but "care" is a more encompassing descriptor pointing to the fact that "healthcare" is not the only thing we do. A whole array of activities happen in the hospital that fit with caring, even without the health context. Whether that's interaction between staff or with patients' families, with doctors, chaplains, volunteers, our community, contractors and suppliers. "Care" is a good descriptor of what we do at the San, encompassing all aspects of our care—not only healthcare.

- **Inspiring**

When I think about this word in our vision statement, it's about how we can demonstrate to our patients, staff and clinicians that the San is not only delivering a service: we want to motivate and promote hope and wellbeing. We seek to provide our people with an environment in which they can engage with the San's values. For example, we talk about continuity—one of our core values—which means that, beyond this acute episode of care, what are the things we can do to add value to the services we provide so we can help people continue to live well, to make good choices about their health and experience greater wellbeing into the future.

We want to inspire our staff and patients to see that care extends beyond the period of hospitalisation, and that the San cares what happens to people beyond a particular test or procedure. We want to provide not only the inspiration and motivation but also the facilities and services, so patients can continue to do well long term.

- **Hope**

One aspect of hope is confidence. People should feel confident that when they place themselves or their loved ones in the care of the San, they feel safe and assured that they will be well looked after. We want people to feel confident that each person will do their best to provide good care, whether it's the front desk staff, the cleaning staff, the people who prepare meals, the nursing staff, clerical staff, clinical staff, doctors, administrative staff, finance staff, maintenance staff or volunteers.

We encourage our staff to reflect on how they'd feel if they or their loved ones were in the vulnerable position of being a patient: reliant on others for accurate diagnosis and information, for treatments and surgery, or their basic day-to-day needs. It is an enormous responsibility for us as we deliver that care and look after their needs to the best of our ability.

Another layer to "hope" is biblical hope. To have a sure anchor of the soul, a hope and trust grounded in the Word and promises of God. To have confidence that during and beyond this episode of hospitalisation, pain, difficulty or grief, there is comfort and hope, that our lives have meaning and purpose, and that we are valued.

- **Wellbeing**

Wellbeing can be defined as a state of balance or alignment in the body, mind and spirit. This has such a close link with the San's mission: "Christianity in Action—caring for the body, mind and spirit of our patients, colleagues, community and ourselves." We want wellbeing for all of these people; we want them to flourish, to be resilient, to feel safe and connected.

A phrase used since early on in the organisation's history to describe the San is that it's a place "where people learned to live well." We are committed to continuing to do the things we do well,

"Take Me to the San"

and to look for opportunities to enhance what we currently do to further promote wellness and wellbeing.

For the San to thrive

Of course, a vision needs to be put into practice and this has been the key part of our process of strategic planning for the future. In the healthcare sector, we talk about measures around customer satisfaction, customer experience and quality outcomes.

During a stay in hospital, sometimes there is a difference between what is considered a good outcome by the surgeon or the hospital, and the outcome expected by the patient. The San is doing a lot of work in these key areas: Did the patient have a good outcome? Did the patient report they had a good outcome? Were the patient's expectations met? And if not, why not, and how can we better measure and manage that, so there are smaller gaps between the actual and the perceived outcome? This is important for both the patient and the organisation.

Employee engagement is another area the San measures on an ongoing basis, in order to know the things that impede or promote the level of engagement staff have with the organisation. We also measure brand reputation and assess how well known are we in the community and across the main drawing areas for the San. We want to know what people think about the services we provide and how we can continue to improve.

Key financial measures are also part of the total picture. We measure revenue, activity and bottom-line performance. The San is a not-for-profit organisation, which means that any income generated at the San that exceeds the costs to run the business is reinvested back into the San. Reinvesting any profit back into the business allows the San to maintain high standards in its facilities, services and technology, to attract and retain the best staff, and to support and develop people within the organisation. It also helps deliver world-class excellence and care that gives our patients cause for hope and wellbeing, and inspires them that this is where they should come for their care.

Mission Shapes Our Vision for the Future

We need to communicate well with our staff about the balance between providing good patient care, staff workloads, and managing resources and finances. As leaders, we have to genuinely engage with our staff, listen to any concerns or issues, and be able to provide transparent information about budgets. We need everyone to support each other and the organisation. The hospital executives and managers don't have all the answers, but as a collective—and with an engaged and motivated staff—we will find ways to achieve the vision.

We're always looking at ways to move forward and put the organisation in a position to thrive. We never say that we've arrived. We know there are challenges, and we won't shy away from them. We always strive to be open and transparent about challenges, while remaining focused on the many ways we deliver whole-person care.

At the San, we know we have an enormous responsibility to care for the body, mind and spirit of our patients, staff, community and ourselves. We know we are not perfect, but we also know that what we do makes a real and lasting difference.

We have amazing staff, doctors and volunteers who contribute in necessary and unique ways to help us uphold our core values, achieve our vision, and fulfil our mission. With this team working together, the San will continue to develop and deliver wholistic healthcare services that promote lasting wellbeing.

A patient story illustrates the impact of mission-driven, whole-person care at the San. The following is from a letter a patient sent to us in 2018:

> I would like to say thank you and commend the San and its staff who cared for me during my two-week stay for major surgery, which included time in intensive care.
>
> I experienced exceptional skills and care. Being treated with compassion is a huge underpinning for the healing process . . . and this is a direct reflection of the hospital's recruitment, training, management practices and culture.
>
> The staff attitude toward my care has been amazing,

as has been their skills. I have been involved in many scientific and management ventures in my full life, and I am so impressed with the technical care, the communication and the facilities here that I find it difficult to describe. Exceptional comes to mind. My family and I love the San.

My surgery and my experience at the San will not only make my life longer, but it will also make my life richer. . . . This experience has not only been physically transforming, it has been emotionally and spiritually uplifting.

This patient's experience—and millions like it over the past 116 years—is why the San exists. We touch countless lives every year. Our vision for the future—inspiring hope and wellbeing—builds on the solid foundations laid at the San since 1903, based on our mission: "Christianity in action—caring for the body, mind and spirit of our patients, colleagues, community and ourselves."

1. Australian Private Hospitals Association, Media Release: "Public Hospitals Being Privatised by Stealth," December 6, 2017, <www.apha.org.au/wp-content/uploads/2017/12/Public-Hospitals-being-privatised-by-stealth-Media-Release.pdf>.

2. Australian Private Hospitals Association, APHA Analysis Paper 02/2017: "Private Patients in Public Hospitals," <www.apha.org.au/wp-content/uploads/2017/08/APHA-analysis-paper-Private-patients-in-public-hospitals.pdf>.

3. Australian Private Hospitals Association, Media Release: "Queensland Health Minister Masking Deliberate ED Cash Grab," April 24, 2018, <www.apha.org.au/wp-content/uploads/2018/04/Media-Release-Queensland-health-minister-masking-deliberate-ED-cash-grab.pdf>.

4. Australia Institute of Health and Welfare, "Private health insurance use in Australian hospitals: 2006–07 to 2015–16—Australian hospital statistics," 2017, <https://www.aihw.gov.au/getmedia/f95e7fc9-db3f-4e7e-a5f5-38f2f69cd539/aihw-hse-196.pdf.aspx?inline=true>.

5. Australian Private Hospitals Association, APHA Analysis Paper 02/2017: "Private Patients in Public Hospitals," <www.apha.org.au/wp-content/uploads/2017/08/APHA-analysis-paper-Private-patients-in-public-hospitals.pdf>.

6. Australian Private Hospitals Association, Media Release: "Private Patients in Public Hospitals Numbers Up Again," May 17, 2018, <www.apha.org.au/wp-content/uploads/2018/05/17052018_apraMarch_FINAL.pdf>.

Editorial Team

Dr Branimir Schubert—Director of Mission Integration, Adventist HealthCare

Denise Murray—journalist and former San nurse

Nathan Brown—book editor, Signs Publishing

Professor Anthony Williams—university lecturer and editor

Authors and Contributors

Annette Baldwin—former Director of Nursing, Sydney Adventist Hospital

Dr Herbert E Clifford—former Chief Executive Officer, Sydney Adventist Hospital

Dr Alex S Currie—pastor and retired chaplain, Sydney Adventist Hospital

Philip D Currie—former San nurse, manager and former Chief Executive Officer, Sydney Adventist Hospital

Dr Alan Gibbons—former Assistant Director of Nursing and San Nurse Educator, Sydney Adventist Hospital

Brett Goods—former San nurse and manager, current Chief Executive Officer, Adventist HealthCare

Patrina McLean—Manager, San Help Team Volunteers

Dr Warren Millist—former anaesthetist, Sydney Adventist Hospital

Associate Professor Paul Race—academic and lecturer, former San nurse

Rose-Marie Radley—former Director of Nursing, Sydney Adventist Hospital

Dr Branimir Schubert—Director of Mission Integration, Adventist HealthCare

Stenoy (Steve) Stephenson—Chaplain and Manager of Spiritual Care Services, Sydney Adventist Hospital

Healthcare innovation since 1903

Sydney Adventist Hospital has been a leader in healthcare for our community since 1903. We started leading health and wellbeing when we first opened our doors as the 'Sydney Sanitarium' – and we're still fondly known as 'the **San**' today.

We led the way in **maternity** care, not just helping women give birth but helping them become mothers. We led the way with ground-breaking **heart services** in the 1970s and we led the way with the first private 24/7 **emergency** care department in NSW. We are a leader in providing wholistic care for those with **cancer**, and training healthcare workers for the future. Today we're leading the way in **robotic** surgery, with state-of-the-art equipment and extraordinary doctors on our team. But most importantly, over all these years what we've really been known for is our leadership in providing remarkable **care**. Care delivered by trusted teams of experts working together in an environment where only remarkable is good enough.

Remarkable

SYDNEY ADVENTIST HOSPITAL

sah.org.au/remarkable

185 Fox Valley Road Wahroonga 2076
Tel: **02 9487 9111**